SANCTITY AND SIN

SANCTITY AND SIN

The Collected Poems and Prose Poems of
Donald Wandrei

Edited by S. T. Joshi

Hippocampus Press

New York

Introduction and editorial matter
copyright © 2008 by S. T. Joshi

Published by Hippocampus Press
P.O. Box 641, New York, NY 10156.
www.hippocampuspress.com

Text by Donald Wandrei, and artwork by Howard Wandrei,
copyright © 2008 by Harold Hughesdon.

Cover design by Barbara Briggs Silbert.
Hippocampus Press logo designed by Anastasia Damianakos.

First Edition
1 3 5 7 9 8 6 4 2

ISBN 0-9771734-9-6
ISBN-13: 978-0-9771734-9-5

CONTENTS

INTRODUCTION

It is entirely possible that Donald Wandrei (1908–1987) will ultimately be remembered principally for his poetry. In spite of such short stories as "The Red Brain" and "Colossus," and the novel *The Web of Easter Island*, it is Wandrei's verse that is the most consistently meritorious branch of his literary work. This is the more remarkable in that the overwhelming bulk of his poetry seems to have been written in his teens and early twenties. *Ecstasy and Other Poems* (1928) and *Dark Odyssey* (1931) contain the majority of his verse; and of the poems not derived from these collections included in *Poems for Midnight* (1964), most seem to have been written in the very late 1920s and early 1930s. H. P. Lovecraft read the *Sonnets of the Midnight Hours* in manuscript in 1927,[1] although the cycle was not published in its entirety until *Poems for Midnight*—if, indeed, it was published complete there. Why Wandrei stopped writing poetry after about 1934 may be as much of a mystery as his surcease of fiction-writing—or, at least, the publishing of his fiction—at about the same time. How much we have lost may be gauged by the four poems Wandrei wrote in late 1977 and 1978, poems as finely polished as those of his youth.

The central theme of Wandrei's early verse is encapsulated in a line from "Let Us Love To-night": "Beauty must die." This is the burden of the very first poem in *Ecstasy and Other Poems*, "The Voice of Beauty," which flawlessly crystallises this emotion. Even Wandrei's most erotically unrestrained poem, "Ecstasy," slyly introduces this theme amidst its paean to the glories of physical love:

> Now shall I hold her white body closer and closer, till her red lips be ashen . . .

It is this funereal image that lingers over and above the ecstasies of the rest of the poem; and the final lines make it clear what conception Wandrei wishes to leave us with:

> There will never be rapture nor passion like ours, our bound shall not sever
> Though we die.

---

1. Letter to Frank Belknap Long, November 1927; *Selected Letters 1925–1929* (Sauk City, WI: Arkham House, 1968), p. 186.

The poet is wearied of life, which he has drained to the dregs; he has loved too well, seen and read too much, and longs for some fresh impulse to jolt him out of his jaded ennui:

> Weary of pomp and power, gorged with glut,
>   I turn to this,
> And find that what I thought so great is but
>   A maiden's kiss. ("Awakening")

But such moments are few, and he can only yearn for oblivion:

> Out of oblivion, no voice will stir
>   To tell of pomp and splendour long unknown,
>   Of buried kings, and empires perilous;
> The older glory of the days that were
>   Will be as perished poppies overblown
>   In Paphian gardens lost and ruinous. ("Futility")

It is passages like this that introduce the cosmic element so familiar from Wandrei's fiction. The bulk of Wandrei's poetry is, in fact, not horrific but lyric, elegiac (see his exquisite "In Memoriam: George Sterling"), and erotic; and it could be said that Wandrei achieves his most striking effects as a poet when he combines the love poem with cosmicism—a unique compound we can find in no poetry save that of Clark Ashton Smith. "To Myrrhiline" contains an imperishable line, "For thee, the gods a planet would destroy"; from another perspective, the poet in "Borealis" scans the skies, where

> All heaven smouldered in mysterious burning
> And blazed in beauty, deep on topless deep . . .

But the conclusion is arresting:

> And then I turned, and looked within your eyes,
> And all the glory faded from the skies.

Pure cosmicism is manifested in "The Challenger":

> He passed beyond the utmost realm of stars,
> Beyond the heavens' great celestial throng,
> In search of vengeance for an ancient wrong
> Inflicted by the gods in elder wars.
> He burst asunder all the whelming bars
> Of time and space, and strode upon his long
> Abyssal pilgrimage, undaunted, strong
> From all the hate of all those bitter scars.

> Forever mounting past the realm of light,
> He stood at last before the citadel
> That rose from out the gulfs of utter night,
> Malignant, as if guarded by a spell,
> And on the doors of doom, disdainful, hurled
> His cosmic challenge in an alien world.

A slightly different type of cosmicism—one where humanity's limitations in the face of an alien and unknown cosmos is etched—can be seen in "Chaos Resolved":

> So few the days, so much that one could know,
> So little light, so many corridors,
> So dark whichever pathway one may go,
> So great the gap, and firmly barred the doors,
> That I am weary though I've gone not far,
> And find defeat ere I have much begun;
> Wherefor, solution distant as a star,
> And certainty, by doubt and change, undone,
> And conquest everlastingly beyond,
> Where no man walks, and shall not ever see,
> Nor ever have; and since this mortal bond
> Is too exacting for man's magistry,—
> Therefor am I, with what I have, content,
> But still assail the deeper firmament.

The poet, blessed or cursed with an unnatural heightening of sensation, can occasionally find himself monomaniacally fascinated with a single phenomenon, as in the remarkable poem "Red":

> Oh color hideous, appalling, mad,
>   Apocalyptic prophet of our doom,
> Specter, in swathings of sick scarlet clad,
>   Whence came you, spawn of what abysmal womb?

Similarly, in "The Five Lords," who are Black, Green, Red, Purple, and White, each of them is in some fashion connected with death; Black "gave him the pall of Death's last blight, / All things died in my black might"; Green is the colour of "Hatred and spleen," but also of "green corpses"; Red, the colour of blood, is "a spectre from the dead"; Purple has "royal robes like a purple ghost"; and finally White:

> I am the colour yet to be;
> All his great love will end in me,

In my design;
I am the sweet close winding-sheet
In whose oblivion we shall meet;
Though ye colours pass, though his limbs be fleet,
He is mine.

It is therefore not surprising that a number of Wandrei's poems were inspired by pictorial art, in particular that of his brother Howard Wandrei. This makes particularly poignant the sentiment expressed in an early poem, "The Greatest Regret":

Ah, God, that I could draw instead of write,
That I could picture worlds I've never known,
And wander in far lands and seas, alone,
That I to cosmic realms could take my flight!
Then, on this paper now so blank and white,
The growth of seeds of morbid beauty, sown
Upon the moon, I'd show, strange things that moan,
And fearful regions of a nameless fright.
With mad new colours and queer lines I'd trace
Phantasmal things of beauty and of death,
Vampirish beings of a stellar race,
Soft plants and creatures, dead, that still draw breath.
Ah, God! That I had genius, mad and great,
To paint the things I never shall relate.

It is as if words were somehow too heavy, too connected with rational discourse to serve as the vehicles for the ethereal sensations expressed in poetry and art:

There is a language I would fain employ,
An unknown golden tongue where every word
Is like the pure, sweet warbling of a bird,
And every sound a thing of lyric joy.
That tongue hath no harsh syllable to annoy
The listening ear; its tones are softly heard
As if a wind had musically stirred
Far silver bells with Song's most sweet alloy.
And I, who long for fairer melodies
Would use that tongue's undreamed-of ecstasies
For songs as wondrous as this wondrous dream,

Whose perfect euphony would be as clear
    And haunting as some fabulous lost stream,
Poems for Beauty's own enraptured ear.
                             ("The Poet's Language")

Of the horrific poetry, perhaps Wandrei's single most celebrated—or no-torious—poem is "The Corpse Speaks." Blunt and obvious as this is, it is nonetheless effective:

Dark, dark, cold, dead,
Silent, still, old, dead;
Dead, dead,
For ever dead.
Dead, dead,
For ever dead.

Flesh? Fled.
For ever fled.
Body? Spread.
For ever spread.
Soul? Dead.
For ever dead.
For ever dead, dead, dead.

Rarely have monosyllables been used to such harrowing effect. They suggest all manner of things—the ultimate decomposition of the human brain in death; the hammering of nails in a coffin; the slow, monstrous march of zombies. No other diction, no other imagery, no other metre could convey quite this effect.[2]

More conventionally, many poems transport us to lands of wonder and fantasy where realism is sloughed off and imagination rules:

For many a thousand leagues about
    Terrific things hold fearful sway,
    That war eternally on day
And change the name of Night to rout.
    . . .

---

2. Steven J. Mariconda points out to me that the mechanical repetition of "dead" may have been derived from "The Grave" by the obscure poet Park Barnitz, whose *The Book of Jade* (1902) Wandrei wished to show Lovecraft at the John Hay Library when he visited Lovecraft in 1932 (see Lovecraft's letter to James F. Morton, 21 September 1932; *Selected Letters 1932–1934* [Sauk City WI: Arkham House, 1976], p. 69).

Upon that distant evil star
                They hold in mirth their mad domain,
                And antique wizards try in vain
To slay the fiends in magic war.
                                ("In Mandrikor")

"Somewhere Past Ispahan," Wandrei's longest single poem, elegantly unites many of his poetic themes—fantasy, eroticism, the ennui of exhausted sensation—in a kaleidoscopic panorama of all that the world and the universe have to offer to the sensitive mind:

                Now I am bored with all things brief and transitory,
                With love, and life, and death, and even with ennui;
                Now no things interest me,
                And I am sick alike of passion and of glory,
                Of days and nights that are an old and tiring story,
                And dreams that can not be.

To a consciousness like this, only an escape into the imagination can offer solace:

                Into the moonlight, Cyrenaya, I would go
                And leave behind me all the weary works of man,
                And take the caravan
                To heart's desire that only I and Allah know,
                The outer-lands where all's a dream, and dream-winds blow
                Somewhere past Ispahan.

Wandrei's most extensive venture into horrific verse is the *Sonnets of the Midnight Hours*. Here we become concerned both with origins and with Wandrei's final wishes for this sequence. In *Ecstasy and Other Poems* we find the poem "Nightmare"; revised, this appears as "Nightmare in Green" in the *Sonnets of the Midnight Hours*. I am inclined to think that—as with Lovecraft's "Recapture," written several weeks before *Fungi from Yuggoth* but ultimately incorporated into that cycle—"Nightmare" was written prior to the bulk of the other sonnets and may have suggested the framework of the rest. Then there is the question of what the final version of the *Sonnets* should be. Three different versions were published in Wandrei's lifetime: twelve sonnets appeared in various issues of *Weird Tales* between May 1928 and March 1929; twenty appeared in August Derleth's anthology *Dark of the Moon* (1947); and finally, twenty-six appeared in *Poems for Midnight*. Here is a conspectus of the appearances:

Sonnet	Weird Tales	Dark of the Moon	Poems for Midnight
The Hungry Flowers	■	■	■
Dream-Horror	■	■[3]	■[3]
Purple	■	■	■
The Eye	■	■	■
The Grip of Evil Dreams	■	■[4]	■[4]
As I Remember	■	■[5]	■[5]
The Statues	■	■	■
The Creatures	■	■[6]	■[6]
The Head	■	■	■
The Red Specter	■		
Doom	■		
A Vision of the Future	■	■[7]	■[7]
After Sleep		■	■
In the Attic		■	■
The Cocoon		■	■
The Metal God		■	■
The Little Creature		■	■
The Pool		■	■
The Rack		■	■
Escape		■	■
Capture		■	■
The Bell		■	■
The Unknown Color			■
Monstrous Form			■
Nightmare in Green			■
What Followed Me?			■
Fantastic Sculpture			■
The Tree			■

Many of the sonnets have been revised almost beyond recognition after their initial appearances, to the point that one wonders whether they can even be called the same work. (Compare what was published in *Weird Tales* as "The Creatures" and in *Poems for Midnight* as "The Prey.")[8] The version published

---

3. As "In the Pit."
4. As "The Old Companions."
5. As "The Torturers."
6. As "The Prey."
7. As "The Ultimate Vision."
8. Steve Behrends has directed me to a letter by Wandrei to August Derleth (27 No-

in *Poems for Midnight* differs from that in *Dark of the Moon* by the addition of six sonnets and also by an extensive rearrangement of the others. Ultimately, the *Poems for Midnight* text must be regarded as Wandrei's final version; no doubt he failed to retain the two uncollected sonnets from *Weird Tales* ("The Red Specter" and "Doom") because he did not think them worthy of inclusion. Still, I would give much to read the manuscript of the *Sonnets* mentioned by Lovecraft in 1927.

What, then, are we to make of the *Sonnets of the Midnight Hours?* They are in one sense more unified than Lovecraft's *Fungi from Yuggoth* in that all are narrated in the first person and that they all, evidently, were inspired by actual dreams of Wandrei's; but they lack even more than Lovecraft's any overriding philosophical purpose or aim. As poetry designed to send a shudder up the spine they are undeniably powerful; but not a single one of them has any other function but to horrify.

The degree to which Wandrei revised his verse has just been touched upon; but I want to cite two further examples that show how Wandrei, in recasting a poem, could change its entire philosophical and aesthetic message. I have already cited "The Voice of Beauty" from *Ecstasy;* compare this now with a revised version, now titled "The Dream That Dies":

> Like a creature unseen as it scurries and passes
> With whispering steps through the wildwood grasses,
> Like the ghost of an echoing note
> From a meadowlark's passionate throat,
> Like the rustle of small
> Blown petals that fall,
> Desolate, lonely, and far
> As a cindering star,
> Like the sound of the sea or the rain,
> Murmur of all things that wane,
> Like foam in a tempest scattered and thinned
> Or vanishing leaves that drift off with the wind,
> Like a mist that fades into sodden skies
> Is the dream as it dies.

Whereas the first version connects with Wandrei's early theme of the transitoriness of beauty, the second has a substantially different connotation.

---

vember 1945; State Historical Society of Wisconsin) in which he discusses the revision of these sonnets: "I've been at the SONNETS OF THE MIDNIGHT HOURS the past week-end; there were 26 in all, but unless some of them can be greatly improved, they will be reduced to 20 or 22. I have made revisions on all but 4 or 5."

Much of the death-imagery of the original has been eliminated or muted; even so simple a change as "meadowlark" for "nightingale" in the fourth line is momentous, the latter suggesting mourning, the former not.

A similarly startling transformation occurs in the poem called "Death and the Poet" in *Ecstasy* and "Death and the Traveler" in *Poems for Midnight*. Although the two versions begin similarly—Death offers the other the boons of his kingdom—they end very differently. In *Ecstasy* we read:

DEATH: Ah Poet, scorn me not,
    For this I offer thee: Hast thou forgot
  The face that haunts thy memory?
  The soft, red lips? The shadowy eyes?
  The mortal flesh that dies?
    Oh Poet, this I offer thee,
  Thy one Beloved fair and sweet,
  In whom all Beauty's graces meet—

THE POET (*wildly*): I yield! I yield! Thy lips, Oh Death!

Here the poet cannot withstand the temptation to unite in death with his lost beloved. In *Poems for Midnight* this becomes:

DEATH: Ah Traveler, scorn me not
  For I will help you find—
  Have you forgot?—
  The face that haunts your heart and mind.
  In my domain alone you'll capture
  Your soul's desire, all lasting rapture,
  All past and future. Traveler, stay!

TRAVELER: Not now, not yet. I go my way,
  I still have far to go, it's late.

DEATH: However far you go, I wait.

TRAVELER: Goodby, but if we meet again—

DEATH: We will. We will, and I know when.

TRAVELER: Not soon for I must find a song—

DEATH: Not long, not long. . . .

The traveler is himself a poet, and the "song" he must find is a symbol for the immortality to be conferred by art. But Wandrei sees this only as a fleeting and temporary thing.

Wandrei's uncollected or fugitive poems reveal a much broader range of tone and subject matter than the poems he chose to collect in his various volumes. Even if we exclude such whimsys (found in letters and clearly not intended for publication) as "The School of Seduction" or the off-colour limerick he sent to August Derleth in 1937, we have such items as "Portrait of a Lady During a Half Hour Wait While She Finished Dressing," a delightful bit of sophisticated comic verse, or "Lyrics of Doubt," some of the most deeply pensive philosophical verse Wandrei ever wrote. Four poems published in *Weird Tales* between 1930 and 1932 remained uncollected; one wonders whether Wandrei simply forgot about these works when assembling *Poems for Midnight*, for certainly they reveal no diminution of power or poignancy from the other verse of the period. Other uncollected verse, chiefly humorous or satirical, has been recently discovered among school publications of the University of Minnesota, and each adds its cumulative weight to our understanding of Wandrei's poetic palette.

Wandrei's dozen or so prose poems—the majority of them, as with his verse, apparently written during the period 1925–30, although some were published much later—exhibit many of the same concerns as his poetry. One of the earliest items, "Paphos," is a gorgeous evocation of classical Greece very much in the manner of some of the work of Wandrei's colleagues, Clark Ashton Smith and, especially, Samuel Loveman. The most characteristic prose poems, however, fuse love (and at times eroticism) with cosmicism into a distinctive amalgam; among the most effective of these are "The One Who Died" and "Ebony and Silver." The latter seems to have surprised Wandrei himself (as he testifies in a letter) by virtue of the explicitness of its sexual imagery. Several prose poems are manifestly autobiographical, some seeming to be simple transcripts of dreams. Over all the prose poems one can see the general influence of Clark Ashton Smith, whose *Ebony and Crystal: Poems in Verse and Prose* (1922) remained for Wandrei a kind of aesthetic talisman—the book that appears to have inspired him to creative expression in his late teens.

After a hiatus of about forty-five years (assuming that Wandrei wrote no poetry in this period—we simply have no way of telling whether he did or not) Wandrei returned to poetry in late 1977 and 1978, circulating four poems to friends and colleagues. Perhaps the most remarkable is "I Am Man," which adapts the grotesque metre of "The Corpse Speaks" to produce a quietly pensive philosophical meditation. In a work that simultaneously vaunts mankind's achievements and puts them into cosmic perspective—similar, perhaps, to his tale "Requiem for Earth"—Wandrei has written one of his most unforgettable pieces:

I am man.
I am slayer, I am slain,
I am fire,
I am sod,
I aspire
To play God,
I am the empty brain
Of man I tire.

But although "I am master of each living thing," although "I am the triumph of all-seeing eye," what will it all mean at the end of Time?

Not on earth or anywhere
Will atom keep
In endless deep
Or starfire care
Of right or wrong,
Of why the pain
Or know the song
That once was man.

This is the Wandrei we recognise both as the precocious youth who wrote "The Red Brain" in his teens and as the old man who, although rarely letting his work see print—or even another's eyes—continued to ponder humanity's place in the cosmic scheme of things. What Wandrei's final place in literature will be, it is not possible now to say—the vast bulk of his unpublished work must be printed and studied before we can take full stock of his literary worth. But whatever place he ultimately occupies, his flawlessly chiselled poetry, old-fashioned as it is by current standards, will surely continue to live as a vital and central component of his collected works. Among the Lovecraft circle Wandrei had no superior as a poet save Clark Ashton Smith and, perhaps, Samuel Loveman; and the fact that nearly all his verse could, chronologically speaking, be termed juvenilia makes us wonder what heights he could have achieved, both in prose and in poetry, had he continued to write into his maturity, when philosophical calm would have tempered the white-hot fire of ecstatic youth.

—S. T. JOSHI

A Note on This Edition

This volume collects all known poems and prose poems by Donald Wandrei. The poems are arranged basically as they appeared in Wandrei's three collections, *Ecstasy and Other Poems* (1928), *Dark Odyssey* (1931), and *Poems for Midnight* (1964). Appended are uncollected poems unearthed from periodicals or derived from unpublished manuscripts, followed by prose poems. Some of the latter appeared in *Don't Dream* (1997) and *A Donald Wandrei Miscellany* (2001).

Wandrei was constantly revising his poems, and I have presented his poems in their final form. Eleven poems from *Ecstasy* and nine from *Dark Odyssey* were reproduced in *Poems for Midnight,* where they appeared with significant revision. I have printed the revised versions in the sequence they occupy in *Ecstasy* and *Dark Odyssey*. Sometimes Wandrei revised his poems so radically that they can be regarded as different poems; in those cases both versions are presented, each in the sequence it originally occupied.

I would like to thank Steve Behrends, John D. Haefele, Marc A. Michaud, David E. Schultz, Richard L. Tierney, and the librarians of John Hay Library of Brown University for assistance in gathering these poems. Thanks also to Dwayne Olson, representative of the Estate of Donald Wandrei.

ECSTASY
AND OTHER POEMS

In Memoriam:
No Name

THE VOICE OF BEAUTY

Like the voice of a wind that shivers and passes
With whispering steps through the willow-grasses,
Like the pain in a passionate note
From a nightingale's golden throat,
Like the voiceless cry   5
Of flowers that die,
Desolate, lonely, and far,
Like a perishing star,
Like the wind, and the trees, and the rain,
That murmur of things that wane,   10
Like the rows of poppies scattered and thinned,
Or the rustle of leaves that drift with the wind,
Like a mist that fades in the sodden skies
Is the voice of Beauty that dies.

SONG OF AUTUMN

Oh, spring is gone
And summer is fled,
Oh, the nights are long
And the days are dead,
And the trees are bare   5
And the skies are lead,
        And the wind is blowing cold.

The days are short
And the days are dark,
Autumn is old   10
And the north-wind—hark!
How it howls and whoops
About the eaves,
How it wildly swoops

The dry dead leaves   15
To their tomb.
And its faintest breath
Has the cold of death
From the Arctic gloom.
And it cries   20
With fitful gust
'Neath the lowering skies
As it stirs the dust
Of summer flown.
The days are drear,   25
And the long nights near
When the cold monotone
Of the wind will moan
Through lone
Fields sere.   30

Oh, spring is gone
And summer is fled,
Oh, the nights are long
And the days are dead,
     And the wind is blowing cold.   35

ECSTASY

I am enraptured of one immortally lovely, with beautiful tresses,
    With beauty of face and of body as the deathlessly beautiful Greek;
I am enraptured by strange and undreamed-of passionate sinful caresses
    That I seek.

The gifts of my body I bring to a flesh-white and beautiful palace,   5
    The passion-born kiss and caress of my maddening desire;
I hold all her body a beautiful living white chalice
    For wine of fire.

She will strip herself naked, in splendid and terrible glory array her,
    A slave of her passion, my passion, our ecstasy secret, malign;   10

The rapture of flesh, and desire, with all strange secrets I will betray her,
        Till her body be mine.

Her lips and her face and her breasts, all her body I will cover with kisses,
        Her eyes will close at my lips on the feverish brow above;
We will pass from rapture to rapture and plumb the most utter abysses   15
        Of our love.

In my arms I will hold her, passive, but I know her flesh will be aching
        For pleasures and joys that she knows not, for a new and monstrous
            delight;
Our desire with breast to breast and body to body we shall be slaking
        All the night.   20

At her feet I have laid the tribute of a burning intolerable passion,
        Of a passion swayed not by reason, a passion ungovernable, mad;
Now I shall hold her white body closer and closer, till her red lips be ashen,
        And her flesh, glad.

The minutes shall wane in delirium, the burning hours pass slowly,   25
        And all the long night her body to mine I shall press;
We shall live in a rapturous embrace, in an endless and holy
        Caress.

I shall teach her the lore of Venus till all her sweet body tremble,
        Till she lie in ecstasy knowing and desiring her sisterhood;   30
We shall love in our passion in strange and ineffable ways and dissemble
        Evil and good.

As the amorous maidens were loved in decadent Rome I shall love her,
        As Sappho of Lesbos was loved in the glory of Greece that is gone;
Her lips with my lips, her passionate body with mine I shall cover   35
        Till the dawn.

Never has woman been loved as I shall love her, never
        Has man known the terrible glory of woman as I;
There will never be rapture nor passion like ours, our bond shall not sever
        Though we die.   40

LET US LOVE TO-NIGHT

Thou shalt die,
  Even as Song and Life and Love,
  Even as one who loves thee, Love,
Even as I.

Thy lips that in the midnight burn,   5
Thine eyes that for strange raptures yearn,
  Thy body fevered with love's desire,
  Thy breasts that seek delight in fire,
To dust and ash will turn.

Even as I, Oh Myrrhiline,   10
  Shall lose all Beauty in the end,
  So shalt thou thy beauty lend
To Death and Time.

A little while,
  And thou shalt go;   15
  Yea, thy lips that softly smile,
Thy cheeks that glow,
  Thy lovely face uplifted now,
  The scented hair above thy brow,
All to death must go.   20

Thy body now so passionate
  Must die;
For ever and ever and desolate,
  Thou shalt lie.

Beautiful maidens have their bed   25
  Where the lilies bloom above;
Beautiful youths have long lain dead
  By the girls they gave their love.

Beauty and Love and Life must die,
  Youth and Song and Joy;   30

For a little while, our life is bright,
For a little while, there is light,
But a moment will come and death destroy
Even the least. Beauty must die.

Never a rose will deathlessly bloom,   35
Never will Beauty escape the grave,
Never will mortal outlive the tomb—
Life is the gift to a slave.

Thou art beautiful, Myrrhiline,
Thou art loveliest of the things I know;   40
But even thou, Oh Myrrhiline,
After a while shalt go.

And I shall join thee, Myrrhiline,
Sleeping beneath the grass;
Every youth and maiden must   45
Yield his body unto dust,
And even so, Myrrhiline,
We shall pass.

Then let us love tonight,
Let us have joy while we may;   50
Let us give over ourselves to delight,
Let us forget the passing of years,
Let us forget vain sorrow and tears
While we say,
The years of the past have long since flown,   55
The flowers of old are overblown,
Lily and poppy and rose are gone,
Petals tremulous with dew at dawn
Have perished in ruinous gardens fair
As the forgotten girls who placed them there,   60
And the song of Beauty for ever dying
Is whispered by the sad wind sighing
For splendour unknown.
The lips of the singers of Greece are still,

Maiden voices are mute; 65
Never again will a dead girl thrill
    To a silent lute.
The past is forgotten, its lips are dumb,
For us the future never will come,
    Only now do we live. 70

So let us love, Myrrhiline,
    And while the fleeting hours away;
And I shall kiss thy warm, soft lips
As one who of strange pleasure sips,
    And I shall play 75
That I am the deathless Greek upon an urn
With lips that to thine own lips burn,
    And never will the present cease,
    And never shall I find release,
But in thine arms, Myrrhiline, 80
    There will be,
    Endlessly,
        Peace.

VAIN WARNING

When thou at the breasts of thy mistress art slaking
    Thy terrible lust,
Remember the days that will come of the breaking
    Of Venus's trust,
When thou thy pleasure and joy art taking, 5
    Remember the dust.

ON SOME DRAWINGS

Orchids, lilies grow exotic in these drawings,
    Poisonous and beautiful and dead;
Strange, grave women dream of some strange pleasure

In their hidden othertime long fled,
Sorrowing and sorrowing for lost days golden,   5
    Vainly recalling old wraiths of memory,
Passionlessly waiting till the spell shall be broken
    Freeing them to follow passion's sorcery.
Heavy-lidded, somber-eyed, sacrosanct and sinful
    Liliths look beyond the sketchbook's leaf,   10
Living in their silence secrets whence no whisper
    Can escape to tell of muted grief.
Enigmatic loveliness of enigmatic figures,
    Enigmatic regions that no eye can know,
Witching, haunted, haunting, mysterious faces   15
    Beckoning to rites forgotten long ago;
Solemn all you picture them, solemn and so luring,
    Slave and queen and dancing-girl, wondrous fair,
Prisoned here in time for evermore remembered,
    Graven deep the riddle of their deep despair,   20
Leave them to enchantment where you left them lingering
    Moonstruck, voiceless, yet their sorceress-eyes agleam,
Waiting, watching till I come and join them where,
    Lost amid their dreamlands, your captured phantoms dream.

SANCTITY AND SIN

All night I lay between the arms of my beloved,
    All night I sought the poisonous fruit of her;
Yea, all the bitter night I sought the bitter rapture,
    The gall that intermingled with the myrrh.

My blood was burning in my veins, and all the torment   5
    Rose and fell and rose through all the Lesbian night;
And she was cool, yet hers was all the passion,
    And all the ecstasy and dolorous delight.

And we were love-sick, yea, and sick with all love's poison,
    The intolerable sanctity of sin;   10

And we were fierce and passionate in our embraces,
    Lest dawn and barren ashes enter in.

For we would keep the pleasure and the torment burning,
    Yea, we would love till all our senses swoon;
For well we knew the holy night must have an ending,   15
    That love and passion weary all too soon.

But all night long we worshipped at our pagan altar,
    All night I bowed before a burning shrine;
And all the love and wondrous beauty of my beloved
    For one intoxicating night were mine.   20

Love's beauty and love's torment and love's fever-kisses,
    Yea, all love's lyric horror all were sweet;
And all the swooning, sick, and ravishing caresses
    That made our veins and pulses wildly beat.

And I was more insatiate with satiation,   25
    More crazed by all the amorous joys thereof;
And still I sought the overpowering drunken rapture,
    The beauty, terror, and the pain of love.

Our worship went beyond our own dim comprehension,
    A choral hymn of mad and sweetest pain,   30
A chant to loveliness and strange, unfathomed glory,
    A mute triumphal song with love's refrain.

Yea, love and more than love were all the long night's portion,
    Till senses reeled, and time and reason fled,
And beauty passed unto its final perfect beauty,   35
    And holy sin and sanctity were wed.

And so I lay between the arms of my beloved,
    All night in worship and in love I lay;
All night I dreamed the one long night would last for ever,
    I dreamed the night would never turn to day.   40

But Time will pass, and Love will pass, and all Love's pleasure,
    For Beauty ever must dissolve and die;
And all the beauty of that night now lies decaying,
    The hymn and song have changed to moan and cry.

Lo, all the later days are long and dull and weary,   45
    The sands of time are thick, the days march slow;
The memory of the elder ecstasy has faded,
    The tale is told of years of long ago.

And now I cry aloud unto the lonely spaces,
    The vacant spaces of the weary night;   50
All night I lay between the arms of my beloved,
    But dawn destroyed our passionate delight.

The years and love are gone, and thou art gone, beloved,
    And weariness of life oppresses me;
No more, no more I know the fierce desire of woman,   55
    For gall and ash are all the ecstasy.

Unto the utter end I worship thee, beloved,
    Unto the end I worship and adore;
Yea, all the barren years that linger in their passing,
    I worship thee and ever worship more.   60

But bitter is the end of love and man's desire,
    And bitter all the poison that it brings;
All night I lay between the arms of my beloved,
    But only an ancient, buried passion sings.

TO MYRRHILINE

Intoxicated with thy loveliness,
    Drunken with beauty and sweet ecstasy,
    Dreaming majestic dreams, I worship thee
As gods might worship Beauty marvellous.
I have been made by thee idolatrous;   5

I close thee, pure and rare as ivory,
The idol in my shrine of ebony,
Dearest of all dear things that I possess.

Thou art as lovely as that ancient queen
 Who ruled in fabulous, forgotten Troy;   10
Lovely as any girl the world has seen,
 For thee, the gods a planet would destroy.
And I, who hold that Beauty is supreme,
Worship thee, knowing that I only dream.

SONG OF OBLIVION

Rest, with the cold ground resting
 In endless repose;
Rest, with the dear things lying
 In life's dead close;
Sleep, with autumn sleeping,   5
 And the tired day;
Sleep, with the white rose that slumbers
 Its white life away;
Dream, with the flowers dreaming,
 On the dead earth;   10
Dream, with the brown grass withering
 In its dearth;
Pass, with all joy that passes,
 Passing in pain;
Pass, with pleasure that fades   15
 As the mist and the rain;
Die, with the leaves that drift
 On the autumnal gust;
Die, with beauty that dies
 In the stirless dust;   20
Forget, with the blown poppies forgetting
 Their flame and their tears;
Forget, with the long, final forgetting
 Of the oblivious years.

IN MANDRIKOR

They dwell in dying Mandrikor
    Where lichens creep on crumbled fanes
    That still preserve dark ancient stains
But all is mute forevermore.

They dwell in wasteland and in night.   5
    Though nothing visible is there
    The presences pass everywhere
More ghostly than the faint starlight.

For many a thousand leagues around
    Unbodied things hold silent sway   10
    While empty cities rot away
And never footsteps tread the ground.

For all is dead, and all is still,
    And underneath the shroud of gloom
    Lie only shards of that dread doom   15
That fell, all Mandrikor to kill.

No traveler crosses now the land,
    The desolation tomblike, sere,
    The dried-up seas, the deserts drear,
The cold apocalypse of sand.   20

Upon the ruined planet dwell
    Just presences, unseen, unknown
    To any save themselves alone,
For none are left the tale to tell.

THE WOODLAND POOL

Into the shadowland I made my way
Where writhing trees loomed tall to shroud the sky,
And baleful boles of strange misshapen growths

Uprose gigantic in the endless gloom,
Where silence ruled yet something waited me 5
And brooded in that vast and soundless grove.
Where all seemed dead beneath the branch-twined roof
Whose gaunt trunks guarded with malevolence
I passed and reached the black pool's rock-strewn edge.
Ringed all around with sentinels that swayed, 10
And hanging creepers that reluctantly
Gave way, the willows five with solemn droop
Trailed countless fingers in the ebon edge
Of that malign, close-hidden ebon pool.
Within those precincts of the spectral night's 15
Dim citadel, all dank and poisonous,
I paused and watched the cryptic waters watch.
The willow branches' languid tendrils sank,
Descending into midnight depths that lurked
Within the pool so fathomless and dark. 20
I peered amid those waters black and still.
I reached my hands down to the cool, wet depths
And by the dark caress was claimed forever,
And in the waters saw my own face drown,
Drowning as willow-fingers drowned, deep—deep— 25

DEATH AND THE POET: A FRAGMENT

Death: I offer thee such dreams
                As thou hast never known;
                I offer thee the moan
           Of Acherontic streams;
                I offer thee the vague, vast Hadean domain 5
                For thee to reign.

The Poet: I scorn thee, Death.
                Thy rotten breath
                     Offends my nostrils, Go!
                     I can not bear thee, Go! 10

34

Death:	Turn not, Oh Poet, wait!
	The poppies of the dead
	Are black and gold and red,
	And in their solemn state,
	My thrones, majestical, imperial, and great,	15
	Await thy kingly head.

The Poet: I scorn thee, Death.

Death:	I offer thee the wealth
	Of all my spectral lands,
	Blue rubies won by stealth	20
	Of dwarfs in deep Lethean sands;
	I offer thee phantasmal gems
	More fabulous than all the gems of fame,
	Strange wondrous jewels and diadems
	With monstrous fires aflame.	25

The Poet: I scorn thee, Death.

Death:	Oh Poet, these I offer thee:
	The songs that Sappho sung,
	And garlands overflung
	By Paphian maids in gardens swallowed of the sea;	30
	The lips of her of Troy,
	The beauty of her immarbled by the Greek;
	The vanished joy
	Of golden voices that will never speak;
	The sound of perished lutes	35
	And silver flutes
	Once lyrical with pagan melody.
	I offer thee
	The glory of
	A thousand and a thousand years ago,	40
	All things that thou dost love,
	All things that thou wouldst know.

The Poet: I scorn thee, Death.

Death:	Ah Poet, scorn me not,	
	For this I offer thee:	45
	Hast thou forgot	
	The face that haunts thy memory?	
	The soft, red lips? The shadowy eyes?	
	The mortal flesh that dies?	
	Oh Poet, this I offer thee,	50
	Thy one Beloved fair and sweet,	
	In whom all Beauty's graces meet—	

The Poet (*wildly*):   I yield! I yield! Thy lips, Oh Death!

SATIATION

I weary of the old monotony of things;
    The song of life is but a tedious, bitter moan;
The years have passed, yet each long year in passing brings
    Ennui alone.

All pleasures I have ever found have been as gall.   5
    All men, all things, all hopes, my burning dreams of fire;
And now at last I crown me with a coronal
    Of dead desire.

In other stars in old, oblivious years I sought
    My destiny, and found what men can never guess;   10
Yet everywhere, in every region, there was naught
    But weariness.

I took the usual pleasures known to all mankind;
    I found or made new pleasures that I shall not tell;
And yet, in all my travels I could only find   15
    My soul's death-knell.

I have made love in normal and eccentric ways;
    The love of girls more strange on stranger stars I won;

My weary mind has travelled all the stellar maze
    Of star and sun.   20

All time and space were mine, and mine was every sky;
    Abysmal secrets, monstrous mysteries, I know;
And I have had terrific grief, and known the cry
    Of bitter woe.

Now I am jaded with my long, complete excess;   25
    Nothing in all the universe is left for me,
And I am sick to death with utter weariness
    And old ennui.

I lived whole cycles of existence; I am wise;
    I know that death itself will never bring release;   30
For ever will I call, and search the frozen skies
    In vain for peace.

IN MEMORIAM: GEORGE STERLING

Beyond the shadows of the shrouded deep
He peered, and in the curtained realms of sleep
He strove to bring a light.
He sought the infinite in life, but now
Among the greater infinite he quests,   5
And death, the great, from whom he held his vow
Has claimed the everlasting vow of him who coldly rests
In night.
He walks where none can know or see,
Alone and far,   10
A lonely traveler on another star,
A dreamer in eternity
Whose dream of old is gone
Before the greater dream whose dawn
Is night.   15
The earth could not contain
His vision, and he peered across the darkling sky

To read the tale of star and sun,
But found no other than the great refrain:
Oblivion.   20
We shall not weep
For him whose mystic sleep
Was self-imposed.
We shall not weep
For him who sought the mystery,   25
The guessless riddle of infinity.
We shall not weep
For him whose sightless eyes
At last are wise
And fixed forever on the shoreless sea.   30
We shall not weep
For he has passed from stage to stage
To solve one dark, strange riddle, a sage
Who asked and answered in a breath
The greatest riddle and though vassal claimed the vassalage   35
Of death.

BACCHANALIA

Twilight upon the hills and woods was dying,
        The air hung slumbrous in the drowsy heat,
When down the hillside came a long, low crying,
        A song of pagan passion, wild and sweet;
And on the wind the strange, low notes kept falling   5
        Till night had cooled the burning winds of day;
And still it seemed as if great Pan were calling
        Nymphs to play.

Far on the hills, I heard the notes of rapture
        Tremble upon the scented air of night,   10
As though sly Pan had used his pipes to capture
        The loveliest girl to give him strange delight;
And over the woods in ecstasy, and swelling
        In lyric passion rose the piper's song,

Above the bacchanal in the forest dwelling　　　　　　15
　　All night long.

What forms were those that through the forest sleeping
　　Danced and revelled amid the olive-grove?
Was it a half-god or a satyr leaping
　　To claim the maid for whose desire he strove?　　20
Upon their brows, forgotten girls were flinging
　　Garlands of rose and violet, and wreaths of vine;
To pagan Pan their passionate lips were singing
　　Love and wine.

The shadows thickened, but a blaze illuming　　　　　25
　　Outlined the revellers dancing through the woods,
Where ancient gods assuaged their lust consuming
　　With nymphs and girls in amorous Bacchic moods;
And still to flushed and heated faces burning,
　　The rapturous music poured in lyric streams　　30
From Pan's wild pipes, the god's own song of yearning
　　Age-old dreams.

There came a sound: Was it a song of gladness
　　For Youth, and Spring, and the woodland feast of Pan?
Or was it the old despairing cry of sadness　　　　　35
　　Of half-gods outcast from the world of man?
Who cared? Once more immortal Pan was playing
　　His pagan pipes for semigod and maid;
And body to body, drunken forms were swaying
　　In the glade.　　　　　　　　　　　　　　　40

From the sea, a wind; the revelry has ended;
　　I hear a moaning in the dreamless trees;
A frantic whisper with the wind is blended
　　Where maidens swoon in midnight ecstasies;
A warning cry—the shadowy forms are shifting:　　45
　　There is a rush of hooves in the break of dawn;
A last, wild note from the distant hills comes drifting—
　　Pan is gone.

AWAKENING

Weary of pomp and power, gorged with glut,
    I turn to this,
And find that what I thought so great is but
    A maiden's kiss.

RED

What nightmare bore you, hateful blight of red?
    What evil source your awful scarlet flood?
Of desolation and the livid dead,
    Whence came your charnel hue of pain and blood?

You flare up in the all-consuming flame,   5
    You drift along the desert's burning sands;
You are the brand that sears, the mark of shame,
    The dripping symbol of a murderer's hands.

Oh color hideous, appalling, mad,
    Apocalyptic prophet of our doom,   10
Specter, in swathings of sick scarlet clad,
    Whence came you, spawn of what abysmal womb?

The poppy yielded you demented dreams,
    Death-fevers mottled you with lurid shades,
Mars poured on you the bane of baleful beams,   15
    You stain vermilion vipers in dank glades.

Oh color of destruction, rage, and lust,
    Foul messenger of war and holocaust,
Symbol of Armageddon, rot of rust,
    You only live when all worth living's lost.   20

HERMAPHRODITUS

Hermaphroditus, loved and lover,
    Swoons in the moonless olive grove;
Over his breasts his fingers hover,
    Over his loins his deep eyes rove.

There touches his body lightly a shiver,   5
    Trembling, he moans on the trodden grass;
Ecstasy pains him with a quiver,
    Tremors across his white flesh pass.

For ever his heart is filled with yearning,
    He seeks to allay the old desire,   10
But only and ever his flesh is burning,
    Where flame greets flame in quenchless fire.

APHRODITE

With breasts of fire, and passionate lips to slake,
    She lies where the Lesbian poppies nod,
Her flesh a torment, her body a rapturous ache
    For the white-limbed god.

Her eyes with longing, her face with fever burns;   5
    The rose and the violet bind her hair;
For a promised trysting, a god long due, she yearns,
    And her body is bare.

AMPHITRITE

Beyond the rocks there are fair bodies with long tresses,
    And arms as sinuous as snakes,
And there are pale, fair faces calling for caresses
    To soothe white flesh that for caresses aches.

Where only the wind and the wide, waste meadows have their home,   5
    The lonely, lovely sea-maidens call,
With bodies flashing in the sounding seas of foam,
    The white-caps and the foam their coronal.

There are strange eyes that beckon, white breasts and bodies crying
    The sea's eternal mystery,   10
And on the salt sea-wind there comes a wild, sweet sighing
    That drifts from the vacant meadows of the sea.

PHILOMELA

A passionate burst of song from a golden throat,
    A rapture in the night,
A lyric ecstasy, a sad, sweet note,
    Pain, and a choral delight;

The clear, pure warble of a nightingale   5
    In the breathless, waiting morn;
A golden throat, a golden song that fail—
    Love, and Death are born.

A DRINKING SONG

The glasses clink for a Bacchic drink—
    What, ho! For the Bacchic brotherhood!
A wine-red toast to the health of the host—
    Song and the Devil and Wine are good!

The table is spread and the flagon red   5
    Contains what a flagon always should!
For the grape's red juice there is just one use—
    Song and the Devil and Wine are good!

To the host! Clink! Clink! Let the glasses chink!
    With a rare old vintage mellowed in wood!   10
For the good of the town, with the spirits—Down!
    Song and the Devil and Wine are good!

AT THE BACCHIC REVEL

A drunken girl where the revellers whirl—
    Flesh and the grape and a wreath of vine!
A girdle that slips from a maiden's hips—
    Lust, and the red, red wine!

A form that clings to a satyr sings,   5
    The rose, the grape, and a god are mine!
A reveller creeps where his leman sleeps—
    Lust, and the red, red wine!

THE CHALLENGER

He passed beyond the utmost realm of stars,
Beyond the heavens' great celestial throng,
In search of vengeance for an ancient wrong
Inflicted by the gods in elder wars.
He burst asunder all the whelming bars   5
Of time and space, and strode upon his long
Abyssal pilgrimage undaunted, strong
From all the hate of all those bitter scars.

Forever mounting past the realm of light,
He stood at last before the citadel   10
That rose from out the gulfs of utter night,
Malignant, as if guarded by a spell,
And on the doors of doom, disdainful, hurled
His cosmic challenge in an alien world.

THE GREATEST REGRET

Ah, God, that I could draw instead of write,
    That I could picture worlds I've never known,
    And wander in far lands and seas, alone,
That I to cosmic realms could take my flight!
Then, on this paper now so blank and white,   5
    The growth of seeds of morbid beauty, sown
    Upon the moon, I'd show, strange things that moan,
And fearful regions of a nameless fright.
With mad new colours and queer lines I'd trace
    Phantasmal things of beauty and of death,   10
Vampirish beings of a stellar race,
    Soft plants and creatures, dead, that still draw breath.
Ah, God! That I had genius, mad and great,
To paint the things I never shall relate.

FUTILITY

What did it matter a thousand years ago
    That in the later days a boy would come,
    And pass, as all things pass, deeming the dumb
Monotony of life an empty show?

What will it matter a thousand years from now   5
    That once a poet lived and loved and died,
    And by a hideous world was crucified
With thorns of loathing on a fevered brow?

Out of oblivion, no voice will stir
    To tell of pomp and splendour long unknown,   10
    Of buried kings, and empires perilous;
The older glory of the days that were
    Will be as perished poppies overblown
    In Paphian gardens lost and ruinous.

Sanctity and Sin

FROM THE SHADOWLANDS OF MEMORY

Was there a goddess in the days of old,
    Most lovely, half satanic, half divine,
    Who cast on me a mystic spell malign,
And bound me with long coils of dusky gold?
Did I embrace her wildly, did I hold   5
    Her body and her rose-red lips to mine,
    And drink her kisses as a priceless wine?
Did I a lovely deathless form enfold?
I do not know. There is an ache that fills
    My mind with longings for some ancient thing,   10
        Some thing I find not though I ever seek.
It slumbers deep beneath the fabled hills,
    It lies where ashen lips no longer sing—
        A phantom of the dead, forgotten Greek.

THE POET'S LANGUAGE

There is a language I would fain employ,
    An unknown golden tongue where every word
    Is like the pure, sweet warbling of a bird,
And every sound a thing of lyric joy.
That tongue hath no harsh syllable to annoy   5
    The listening ear; its tones are softly heard
    As if a wind had musically stirred
Far silver bells with Song's most sweet alloy.
And I, who long for fairer melodies
Would use that tongue's undreamed-of ecstasies   10
    For songs as wondrous as this wondrous dream,
Whose perfect euphony would be as clear
    And haunting as some fabulous lost stream,
Poems for Beauty's own enraptured ear.

NIGHTMARE

And after this, there came to me one green
    With all the dreadful cerements of the grave,
    Who shambled down the midnight's empty pave
With flapping tatters and long talons lean.
And of his face, there was no vestige seen,   5
    And all his flesh to rottenness was slave;
    He leered so vilely, Horror could not save
Itself from horror at those eyes' blind sheen.
And of that thing there came to me a fear
    So great, I clawed my face to bleeding strips,   10
        And turned to flee that corpse's hideous head.
But everywhere I looked, I saw it near,
    And saw it smile, with fleshless, gaping lips,
    For I was his, that horror of the dead.

VALERIAN

To Clark Ashton Smith

Thy purple eyes, Valerian,
    Have known the fungi of the moon,
Have travelled lands Hesperian,
    Have seen the blood-red plenilune.

Thine eyes were at the avatar   5
    Of lizard-gods in Jupiter,
And saw the space-invading star
    That blasted all the worlds that were.

Thine eyes were old when God was born,
    Have seen the fall of many kings,   10
And watched a queen of Saturn mourn
    The death of pale-green bloated things.

Valerian, thine eyes were sick
    To see the Hylots of Calair,
To watch a little creature pick   15
    Tumescent orchids swart with hair.

And thou hast known the azure mist
    That brought to Mirtylon its doom,
And drunk a wine of amethyst
    Fermented in a wizard's tomb.   20

Thine eyes were stricken when they saw
    Orion's mad, metallic queen;
They passed the land where flowers gnaw
    On curious corpses, gold and green.

Thine eyes, Valerian, are full   25
    Of sights and sounds of outer space,
Abomination beautiful,
    The dark star's necrophilic race.

Valerian! Valerian!
    Thy purple haunted eyes are mad   30
With knowledge of the carrion
    That made Serise's red dwarfs glad.

They gazed on stars that now are dust,
    They gorged on wonders vanished, dead,
They saw Mercurial cities rust   35
    Beneath twin moons of livid red.

They saw the mighty Atthla fall
    A thousand million years ago,
And find its cosmic burial
    Where other universes flow.   40

And once thy purple eyes went blind
    With dazzle of a monstrous flame,
And when they oped they could not find
    A star they knew before it came.

Valerian! Thine eyes are filled   45
    With visions of the stellar pits,
The things that mirthful wizards killed
    With torture on their burning spits.

Valerian! Thine eyes are old
    Beyond the age of any sun;   50
Their secrets will remain untold
    Until the last oblivion.

Valerian! Thine eyes shall shut,
    Their purple vision fade and die,
For they are blinded with the glut   55
    Of every age and every sky.

Dark Odyssey

*This little book is affectionately
dedicated to our Mother and to our
Father, whose sympathy is exceeded
only by their understanding.*

LARGO

How all my days are as an aria played
By fumbling fingers, and forgotten soon,
Or as the futile, giant music made
By seas that thunder vainly to the moon;
How all my time is winnowed, leaving husks   5
Wherein no seed nor any fruit are left,
While there remain but few—how few!—brief dusks
Ere I, by night and darkness, am bereft
Of hope; and how my hours are unavailing
To chart the labyrinths of long assailing;   10
And how my love that burns herein so deep
Shall even as my lost days be foredone,
Even as one who hath a quiet sleep,
And hath no waking to no dawn nor sun.

AUBADE

The flowing porphyry
Of thine eyes holdeth me.

Thy face is aureoled
By softer gold than gold.

The beauty of thy features,   5
Purer than earthly creatures',

Is such as gods impart
With supernatal art.

Naught by thy loveliness
Its equal can confess.   10

FATA MORGANA

Through its valleys and its mountains
    I have wandered in spirit,
I have drunk at the fountains
    Of the gods, I inherit
The nectar of their chalice   5
    And the lotus of their leaven,
I have dwelt in the palace
    Of their paradisal heaven.

Now I fully awaken
    On the meads that are rarest,   10
From the way I have taken
    To the star that is fairest;
From the sweep of vast spaces
    And the suns eternal,
Where I entered the traces   15
    Of a dream supernal.

There is magic, there is splendor
    In your eyes, there is rapture
In your lips that were tender
    In the soft, first capture.   20
Of a glory I have drunken,
    In a madness it has perished,
And the old stars are sunken
    And the ways that I cherished.

Shall I wander in the hollows   25
    Where the asphodels are springing?
Or remain by the willows
    Whence the last birds are winging?
Or be bathed in new glory,
    And forget worlds olden?   30
Or from transitory
    Delight be withholden?

But the eyes have no vision,
    And the heart holds its ravage,
And the mind's decision,   35
    Remote, savage,
For nothing suffices
    Except to blind you;—
Or enchantment that entices,
    Where shall I find you?   40

BOREALIS

The Northern Lights crept down with pulsing streamers
Out of the mystical spaces flung beyond,
As if a wizard's wand
Summoned from realms unknown to earthly dreamers
The luminous shadow of the infinite,   5
Skeins of fluctuant color lit
With skirling fires of weird, vast fanes,
And surge of falling flame of far dominions,
And giant fountains pouring down the wide skylanes.
All heaven smouldered in mysterious burning   10
And blazed in beauty deep on topless deep
Where soaring pinions
Could wing no flight
And where the mind's transcendent vision, unreturning,
Itself was lost beyond abysses of the night. . . .   15
And then I turned, and looked within your eyes,
And all the glory faded from the skies.

IN MEMORIAM: NO NAME

(After a pen-and-in drawing by Howard Wandrei)

We buried her in the solemn fall
    With only the withered trees to watch us passing by;

In Memoriam: No Name

We left her staring at the musty pall,
    Her world and sky.

We shivered in the quiet air,   5
    And left her lovely body to oblivion;
We left her far more quiet body lying there;
    Our task was done.

We left no mark to show her grave,
    We only left her body lying still and deep;   10
We left her only to the waiting earth that gave
    Her birth and sleep.

DARK ODYSSEY

I sought it in far lands of timeless travel
    Athwart the circling citadel of stars,
Where only courage of lost hope could ravel
    The secret of eternal avatars.
With scrutiny of systems long forgotten,   5
    And outer, oldest galaxies that wane;
Amid all worlds of time and dust begotten
    I sought, but sought in vain.

Where dwindling monitors of night had sundered
    And perished in the utmost cosmic tomb,   10
Through space's dead debris I wandered, wondered
    What total purpose wrought such total doom;
Where night was like a shroud before an altar
    Before a vaster deep beyond all thought,
And knowing that my quest at last must falter   15
    And end, there too I sought.

I searched the years that hold all things immortal
    And traveled backward past the age of man

To seek some image far behind some portal
     Long crumbled in primordial pre-time's span;   20
In continents and islands that are sunken,
     Where sand and tides on shattered cities roll,
In constellations now to space-dust shrunken
     I sought my spirit's goal.

And farther back, when worlds were in their dawning,   25
     And farther still when life was yet to come,
Still farther back before the stars were spawning
     The spheres that spin of chance the blind and dumb,
Still farther where not even stars were flaring
     In void, in waste, in riddle never guessed,   30
My dreaming eyes kept searching, seeking, staring
     Upon a fruitless quest.

I peered far down the final future ages,
     I watched the universe grow cold and chill;
The scattered symbols of those closing pages   35
     I read, yet on my trail I wandered still;
When time had ceased, when every world was riven,
     No life or mind or trace of vanished lore,
Then only, from those vacant spaces driven,
     I sought beyond no more.   40

Borne onward yet by that same ceaseless yearning,
     Still seeking that which I had never found,
From utmost regions of strange realms returning,
     I watched on earth the littler things around;
In those mysterious lands and alien places   45
     I sought not, nor in worlds that only seem
To be; I thought to find in nearer faces
     The still-eluding dream.

In eerie borderlands I vainly waited
     By cryptic tarns aglow with lethal flame,   50
In shadow-ruled dominions darkly fated
     To perish when my later footsteps came;

The phantom that so greatly I desired
    I sought in maze of sorcery and bale;
And when in closer human haunts I tired,   55
    I saw I still must fail.

I have not found it sleeping or awaking,
    I will not find it till all things shall cease,
And still for this one dream all else forsaking
    I further search with neither hope nor peace   60
Upon an endless path forever going
    Through trackless labyrinths more dark and deep,
I know this all I ever will be knowing:
    The night that brings a sleep.

LOOK HOMEWARD, ANGEL

(After a pen-and-ink drawing by Howard Wandrei)

So long, so far, so distant have you flown
Through all the space of worlds in time and spirit,
Winging your vast way lonely and alone
In search of something lost, but never near it;
So endlessly, so wearily you paced   5
Along star roads with only moonglow paven
Until your birthsite had become effaced,
Eternity between you and your haven;
And longer ways before you yet to wander
Beyond the soaring clouds' infinity;   10
Unknown what goal, if any goal, lies yonder
Where legend prophesied divinity,
Pause, rest, turn back while still your wings are strong,
Look homeward, angel, for the way is long.

UNDER THE GRASS

(After a pen-and-ink drawing by Howard Wandrei)

Secret the roots that enter the ground,
Secret the winds that hollowly pass
Through them and over them—what shall be found
Under the grass?

Deep stems twining around the mandrake,   5
Pebbles and beetles and layers of earth,
And incubi avidly waiting to take
The blood's full worth.

Long are the roots that enter the soil
And twist their sinuous downward course—   10
What shall reward the delver's toil
When he finds their source?

A cool dark pillow, a comforting bed,
Or the open arms, or the eyes of glass;
And a pebble necklace around his head   15
Under the grass.

YOU WILL COME BACK

When all the olden days are over,
    You will come back to me,
        You will return;
Our thoughts will be more sad than death is
    For we will know how love   5
        Died upon birth.

You will come back to me, lost lover,
    Come back with setting suns
        And looted fields;
We will pour ashes from the phials   10

Sanctity and Sin

Under the Grass

That once ran red as blood
    With wine of life.

Dead eyes will greet dead eyes, and ravage
    Of naked hearts, and dust
        Of wasted years;   15
Mute tongues will tell remembered hemlocks
    And unforgotten nights
        Of slow, fierce grief.

You will come back some day, lost lover,
    Come back, come back to me,   20
        You will return;
And we will part, as once we parted
    In separate deaths, so long,
        So long ago.

AFTER BACCHUS, EROS

The roses, crushed, lie scattered everywhere;
    Each drunken reveller has long since gone;
The fire is cold; no fuming censers flare;
    No gleam illumes the hoofprints on the lawn.

For song and laughter, now the wind's regret;   5
    For youth, a ravished poppy's petals blown;
For feast and wine, the grass stained darkly yet;
    For love, the dell where hired maenads moan.

TO LUCASTA ON HER BIRTHDAY

So fair she is that beauty hath no graces
    Upon her to bestow;
Her face is sweeter than those fabled places
    Where asphodels do grow.

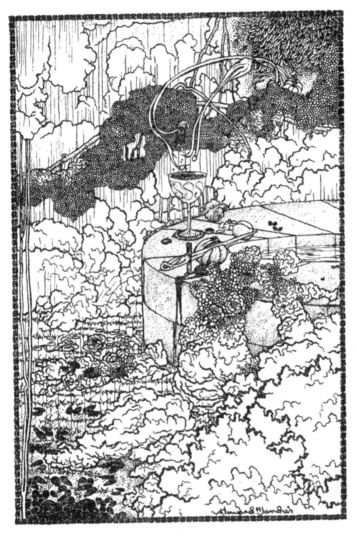

After Bacchus, Eros

Her step is lighter than the summer breezes   5
    That stir the wakened rose;
She walks in charm, adoring nature pleases
    To worship where she goes.

What words convey how closelier she follows
    The storied queens of old?   10
Her garments only know what curves and hollows
    Their gentle drapes enfold.

Be still, O Muse! what syllables soever,
    May sing of her are vain;
Her loveliness in poetry lies never,   15
    For song, not she, doth gain.

VILLANELLE À LA MODE

I promised you a villanelle,
    White poppy of the crimson eve—
Is love so limited, pray tell?

You caught me, bound me, with a spell,
    Enchanted me with dreams that weave;   5
I promised you a villanelle.

Do light thoughts in a light heart dwell,
    And fugues parade from hearts that grieve?
Is love so limited, pray tell?

So little, yet to do so well,   10
    To capture moods that change or leave;
I promised you a villanelle.

Has love become an aquarelle?
    Should love be told in brede or breve?
Is love so limited, pray tell?   15

Not always empty is a shell,
     Nor always full the charming sleeve—
I promised you a villanelle;
Is love so limited, pray tell?

FOR THE PERISHING APHRODITE

Thou hast given me passion, desire, and flame; thou
     hast brought me this feverous love to consume me,
I am drunk with thy spirit, thy body, thy beauty, the
     rapture of endless and awful delight;
Yet the radiance is gone from thy face, is it only the
     refluent glory and glow that relume thee,
Is it only a mirror for love that I find in the beauty
     that else were as shadowed as night?

I have riven all darkness to find thee,   5
I have sundered the stars away;
Was it only for darkness to blind me,
For a love that was fleeting as day?
Like a priest at a shrine I adore thee,
Like a drinker of chloral I dream,   10
Art thou only a phantom before me,
Of the phantoms that are not, but seem?

In the years of the past, in the coming and passing of
     lovers and love and the paths love has taken,
There was never love greater than mine, so destroying,
     so ravaging, ravishing, rapturous, deep;
In the years yet to be, in the slumbering lovers and
     loves of the future, the passions to waken,   15
Will a woman be born, or a man ever live through
     whose soul such a madness and fury will sweep?

I have burned all my flame at the altar,
Was the tribute then given in vain?
Mine the love that can fade not or falter,

Is it thine that shall weaken and wane?　　　　　　　　　　　20
Like a flame, like a splendor supernal,
In a furnace of ecstasy whirled,
As the stars are, my love is eternal,
And its death is the death of the world.

Thou hast webbed me with wonder and yielded me
　　rapture of soul; is it passion or poison I cherish?　　　　　25
I am drugged with delirium, burning with beauty,
　　intoxicate, meshed in the love thou hast sown,
Thou hast woven a spell, was the chantment for only
　　a moment ere worship and love were to perish?
Ere the flame was to fade from thy face, and my love
　　to consume and increase and devour alone?

Wine of life and of death I have drunken,
On the nectar of love I have fed,　　　　　　　　　　　　30
Is the rose to be withered and shrunken?
Shall the poppy be flameless and dead?
Yet it seems that a veil rises slowly
And conceals like a curtain the shrine,
With its drapery hiding all wholly,　　　　　　　　　　　35
And the form that it covers is thine.

MORNING SONG

There is a faint, far rapture of birds in the breathless beauty of dawn,
There is a stir of wakening winds that whisper across the lawn,
And a presence of something supernal drifts over the spring-sweet earth,
And the bitter sleep and the sadness have fled in a strange rebirth.

Oh love, there is terror and pity and peace in the gray soft luminous mist,　5
The grasses with glimmering dew are jewelled in opal and amethyst,
The world is wondrously quiet, so quiet, prophetic of day,
And my heart is fulfilled of its dream as I walk my enchanted way.

Sanctity and Sin

THE WHISPERING KNOLL

(After a pen-and-ink drawing by Howard Wandrei)

There where the gnarled limbs twisted
From a trunk, that withered, blighted bole,
I crawled like one impelled on ways resisted,
I saw the whispering knoll.

Strange was the night, and stranger   5
This hill, haunted by a deathly spell,
Witch-forms tormented, from dark demon danger,
Fore-glimpse of after-hell.

I thought I heard the eerie
Anguish of some lost thing's cry or call   10
While ghostly presences writhed wan and weary
In night's eternal pall.

And mistily shone the ghostly
Moon, if moon-made they, those drifting shapes
And phantoms that seemed hopelessly and lostly   15
In search of closed escapes.

Then dreamlikely they uttered
A sibilance that followed as I stole
Away; the specters by the gnarled trunk muttered
Upon the whispering knoll.   20

THE FIVE LORDS

Black

I was the first to tinge his pen;
I was the only colour when
        He was half-mad;
I brought him dreams of eternal night,

The Whispering Knoll

I gave him the pall of Death's last blight,   5
All things died in my black might,
     Great joy he had.

Green

Once he was pale with love of me,
His sunken eyes could only see
     Emerald green;
For green corpses he did lust,
For sick flames and the crawling dust,   5
He had dreams and thoughts of just
     Hatred and spleen.

Red

I am the colour deep blood-red,
Risen a spectre from the dead
     For his mad eyes;
He was possessed with my red flame,
My Lust, and Fury, and crimson shame,   5
All colours else were wan and tame,
     I, Paradise.

Purple

Fourth was I in the coloured host,
My royal robes like a purple ghost
     Clad him alone;
With power he grew intoxicate,
I was the sign of royal state,   5
Of the mad matriarch who sate
     On a purple throne.

Chorus

We were the colours that his love
Made mad songs and patterns of,
     We were most high;
From each of us he took his joy,
Yet we like a woman came to cloy,   5

We were won and lost of a mad young boy,
  And then passed by.

White

I am the colour yet to be;
All his great love will end in me,
  In my design;
I am the sweet close winding-sheet
In whose oblivion we shall meet;   5
Though ye colours pass, though his limbs be fleet,
  He is mine.

LOST ATLANTIS

Lost Atlantis slumbers deep,
Sunk beneath the washing wave;
Fishes swim and monsters creep
Where its buried cities sleep
In the dark sea-grave.   5
Memories only wander where
Sea-tides ebb and flow;
Only slimy creatures stare
On the cities sleeping there
Since ten thousand years ago.   10
Sunken walls of crumbling stone
Whisper of the days of old
When Atlantis stood alone
And its glory far was known,
By forgotten poets told.   15
But the gulf is cold
On Atlantis dreaming, dreaming
Of the splendor known no more;
Only fishes keep a seeming
Watch upon the ruins gleaming   20
On the sunken shore.
Fronds from out its temples rise;

Seaweed fills deserted lanes;
Shadowy growths and shadowy skies
Mark where dead Atlantis lies   25
With empty fanes.
Phosphorescent creatures go
Swimming through Atlantis doomed;
Only phantom poppies blow,
Only spectral lilies grow   30
Where the fabled roses bloomed.
Tides around Atlantis sweep,
But no voice shall speak again
In the streets now covered deep,
For a long and mystic sleep   35
Lies upon the dead drowned men.
Only growths and fishes dwell
In the depths of gloomy murk;
Time has tolled a solemn knell,
Lost Atlantis slumbers well   40
Where the strange sea-creatures lurk.

THE NIGHT WIND

I hear low whispers from the reeds and rushes,
    Faint footsteps in the willow-bed,
And there are dim, vague rustles in the bushes,
    Like footsteps of the dead.

Is it the wind that stealthily and softly passes   5
    Among the sedges whispering,
Whose hollow steps stir all the river grasses
    To light, low murmuring?

I only know that all the reeds are crying
    A tale of loneliness and woe,   10
That in the grasses there are voices sighing
    For nights of long ago.

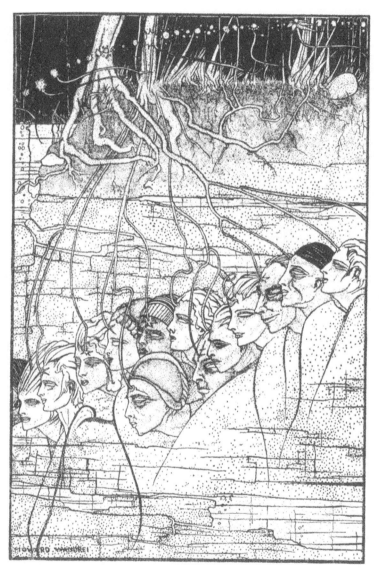

The Night Wind

THE VOYAGERS' RETURN TO TYRE

As we strode the streets of Tyre
The city rang with joyful call
Of those who came to praise this day
And celebrate our festival.
Revel and welcome, games and play   5
Awaited us, sea-weary all,
As we strode down the streets of Tyre.

The sun lay warm along our way,
A heady fragrance filled the air
From flowers strown upon the ground   10
While maidens lovely, smiling, fair,
The garlands from their brows unbound
And cast them for our footfall where
The sun lay warm along our way.

One old familiar face I found   15
Of those the days before the quest.
"Greetings!" I cried but in the throng
The face was lost and I had guessed
As we, triumphant, strode along,
It knew me not from all the rest,   20
One old familiar face I found.

Sunlight and seawind, laughter, song,
And everywhere the women flinging
The wreath, the garland, and the rose,
Hetaira, matron, virgin bringing   25
Gifts that repaid our journey's woes,
And over all a choral singing,
Sunlight and seawind, laughter, song. . . .

THE PLAGUE SHIP

(After a pen-and-ink drawing by Howard Wandrei)

From the stricken hosts of those plague-filled coasts
We turned and set forth once more,
But we turned too late and we knew our fate
Before we had lost the shore.

For the plague germs fed on the sick and the dead   5
And the living walked less like men
Than shadows that crept with the sun, and slept
When the night came down again.

In the distance sank the coast in the dank
And stifling tropic heat;   10
There could not be so still a sea
On which such sunfire beat.

The twilight brought no ease from the hot
Inferno, to the waves
That almost hissed or the shimmering mist   15
That hung on our deep sea-graves.

While sick men stoked, the black hulk poked
Her bow toward the cleaner west
Till the engines failed and we lay there gaoled
By the legions of the pest.   20

Then ocean received the husks that we heaved
From heat and plague as they died,
And one by one with the setting sun
The shadows slipped from our side.

The Plague Ship

CHAOS RESOLVED

So few the days, so much that one could know,
So little light, so many corridors,
So dark whichever pathway one may go,
So great the gap, and firmly barred the doors,
That I am weary though I've gone not far,   5
And find defeat ere I have much begun;
Wherefor, solution distant as a star,
And certainty, by doubt and change, undone,
And conquest everlastingly beyond,
Where no man walks, and shall not ever see,   10
Nor ever have; and since this mortal bond
Is too exacting for man's magistry,—
Therefor am I, with what I have, content,
But still assail the deeper firmament.

EPITHALAMIUM

What though you walk by Mammon unattended,
Or purple, dear to children of the dust,
Or gold that never yet no man befriended,
Or gilded idols undeserving trust,
Yet do you leave the dark and lonely waste   5
With olden dead endeavor all erased,
And years of striving in one moment ended.

These, these are gone, nothing of them remains
Except the fair, faint dream of beauty slowly
Emerging into light from shadowed fanes,   10
And into more than light, to something wholly
And crystal clear, of life and love and rapture,
Beauty more vital for your hearts to capture,
A fuller dream replacing that that wanes.

For all things die, but they die most regretful   15
That flowered not, and all things weep to die,
But they whose life was barren are most fretful,
And they who merely lived are first to sigh;
But fulness leaves no unassuaged desires,
And to no futile dream of death aspires,   20
And of no emptiness is unforgetful.

No love endures if love be only passion
And no love lasts if love be only mind,
Two loves, two deaths, two flameless fires, ashen,
Unless in deeper love both are combined;   25
Then flesh and spirit, unceasing springs, uncover—
Oh sweet beloved and enchanted lover—
The ever fresh design of your own fashion.

Then live! Live in this dual love, partake
Of the dual flower that alone endures;   30
What though one kingdom each of you forsake,
A greater wealth your greater love assures
You, and you leave the aimless labyrinth
For fields of asphodel and hyacinth,
In sunlight splendid meadows to awake.   35

Surely shall Aphrodite give you greeting,
And Psyche hover on the summer air,
And sprites invisible attend the meeting,
And all the laughing nymphs that make earth fair;
Of water, fire, earth and air attend you,   40
The elements their four-fold essence send you,
Treasure outlasting cities fair but fleeting.

And by your side, in beauty's own rebirth
Of pagany, divinely young Apollo,
In your steps on the wakened ways of earth   45
With soft, light golden limbs to dance and follow,
Oh love consummate in the flesh and sprit,

That doth the icon and the dream inherit,
Than which no love can have supremer worth.

Then live! Live with the green, lush trees returning   50
To fulness in the drowsy summer noons,
And deeper fires, burning, burning, burning,
Till beauty into perfect beauty swoons;
Live with all things of earth and airy splendor,
Oh love compassionate and strangely tender,   55
Oh hearts encysted in supernal urning.

Oh light that never shone for me one ray,
Oh bells that shall not ever ring for me,
Shine bright, ring out, attend the sweet assay
Of them, bound, yet magnificently free;   60
Let one long, lingering note through night come stealing,
Symbol of beauty, love, and life, and healing,
Of Hymen and the gods that watch your way.

EPILUDE

There was none before you,
        There will be none after,
I adore you,
        Only you.
There will spring no laughter   5
        Spontaneous as yours,
        Thus I close my doors
For there will come none after,
        After you.

POEMS FOR MIDNIGHT

PHANTOM

She walks with stately grace.
    Her grave, gray eyes a beauty hide
        That has no counterpart in lands of time
Or space;
    And in her movements, languid charms abide.   5

A gray dusk mists the air
    But never changes, never fades,
        And neither dawn nor darkness shades her clime.
No glare
    Of sun illumes the mouldy balustrades.   10

There are no eyes to see,
    No voice to tell of days that were,
        No ears to hear her footsteps die away.
The three
    Old prophecies alone accompany her.   15

She walks with dust and dreams.
    All else is still the realm around,
        And she alone has beauty, grave and gray.
She seems
    A phantom of a kingdom of no sound.   20

THE CORPSE SPEAKS

And I am dead.
Six feet deep I lie,
And I am dead.
I can not close an eye,
I can not move a thigh,   5
I can not even sigh

For I am dead.
Set, fixed, immovable my head;
Set, fixed, immovable my bed;
Set, fixed, immovable myself, now wed   10
To coffin, earth, the dead.
All the rottenness, I dread;
All the flesh on which fat worms have fed;
All the slime and mould that slowly spread
About me, who am dead.   15
Never more shall I hear sound
In my tomb beneath the ground,
In my grave beneath my mound.
Six feet deep my corpse lies, drowned
In dissolution's rot. Around,   20
Eternal night, and earth damp, black, and cold
That presses on my grave and me, rolled
In my own decomposition. Thick white worms have lolled
Their dripping tongues from my soft flesh that, old
And spoiling, lured them. But I could not squirm   25
When I felt through me spread the germ
Of worm that multiplied on worm
Until my dead flesh stirred. I only lay,
Sick, still, and weary, while they ate their way;
I only sighed to feel them play   30
And wriggle through my gray
Corruption. Six feet deep
I lie in my last sleep;
Six feet deep.
I feel the worms that creep, creep, creep,   35
I feel the worms that leap
In ecstasy to reap
The harvest, and to revel deep
In dark liquescence. Mocking maggots peep
At me and slyly chuckle while they keep   40
Their festful riot in my rotting heap.

I now have ceased to bloat;
Worms now have ceased to gloat,

Or in my dead flesh foul to float,
Forevermore.   45
Stained is the coffin floor
Forevermore.
My corpse was once a festering sore
And rotten in each swelling pore,
And rotten to the very core,   50
But now that time is gone of yore
Forevermore.
My body will not pour
A noisome pool as once before.
My bones are hoar   55
Forevermore.
Dark, dark, cold, dead,
Silent, still, old, dead;
Dead, dead,
For ever dead.   60
Dead, dead,
For ever dead.

Flesh? Fled.
For ever fled.
Body? Spread.   65
For ever spread.
Soul? Dead.
For ever dead.
For ever dead, dead, dead.

THE WOMAN AT THE WINDOW

(After a pen-and-ink drawing by Howard Wandrei)

Beyond the window's tracery
        Of arabesques the blood-red sun,
Amid a realm of sorcery,
        Stares with an eye she can not shun.

The Woman at the Window

Out of the window's smouldering red 5
    In all the years by time begun,
With that wild color overspread,
    Her face has watched the dying sun.

She scans the shadows of her land,
    The crimson, never-setting sun, 10
The blood-red waving wastes of sand
    That her domain has overrun.

Ever the orb's fantastic glare
    Of burning, baleful scarlet spun
Meets the mysterious woman's stare 15
    Locked fast with that hypnotic sun.

Till darkness falls—it never will—
    Her vigil never will be done:
Her timeless vision staring still
    Beyond the lifetime of the sun. 20

SHADOWY NIGHT

Shadowy night and the world to cross—
    Why are the marsh-weeds drooping low?
An unseen step on the creeping moss—
    Why has the night-wind ceased to blow?

Shadowy night and the world to cross— 5
    Never a light to mark the trail
But spectral flame on the puff-pod floss
    And the stars in the drowning pools are pale.

Shadowy night and the world to cross—
    Is it the willows shiver and sigh? 10
The tarns run red where the fen-fires toss—
    Why do the mandrakes fear to die?

THE WORM-KING

In a fabulous land, in a fabulous time,
There lived and there ruled on a crumbling throne
A worm that was born of the deep sea-slime,
Whose white fat folds were covered with grime,
And it ruled alone.   5
Not a creature lived in all the land,
And the little red eyes in the serpent's head
Saw only a realm of wet black sand
And the slimy things of the slimy dead
Of its cold sea-tomb.   10
Not a thing disputed the lordly worm
Where it lived and ruled in the endless gloom,
Nor ever a hand caressed its fat;
Through its foul dead realm were it ever to squirm,
All it would find was a plump drowned rat   15
And dead men's bones.
As deathless and old as the deathless sea,
As deathless as ever a worm can be,
And the worm is king for eternity,
It reigned on its multiple thrones.   20
But the musty tale can never be told
Of the realm that rose from stale sea-waves,
Of the white worm-king and the fat white fold,
Of the pulpy head that never grows old,
For the tale is the grave's.

WATER SPRITE

(After a pen-and-ink drawing by Howard Wandrei)

Laughing, she flashes down the shifting tides of green,
Or whirls
Where the rippling waters ebb and flow between
Her coral isles and shadowy pearls
That glimmer beneath her sunless, wind-departed skies.　　　5
Sometimes her gleaming eyes
With beauty of frail and waving fronds go wide,
Sometimes she dreams to music of murmuring waves
That tremble and fall in tide on foaming tide,
Or rests where an ocean current laves　　　　　　　　　　10
The rocks on a sunken shore.
Sometimes in cool delight she floats on drifting weeds
Where breakers and lonely waters roar,
Or speeds
To capture an errant eel　　　　　　　　　　　　　　　15
That enters her wide domain.
From dawn to dusk her white sides feel
The rush of waves that seek in vain
To capture a breast, to hold the hair
That streams from her glowing body bare　　　　　　　　20
Till at last, in her caverned halls
Where sea-friends dwell,
She falls,
And sinks to sleep in a sounding shell.

INCUBUS

She has yielded to the kiss of night,
　　She slumbers lightly here,
All her dreaming, raptured face is white,
　　She dreams of fear.

Water Sprite

There is pressure on her blood-red lips,   5
    Her eyelids vaguely stir;
Are these shadows, now, like finger-tips,
    Caressing her?

On her brow the moonbeams lie as lace,
    No other form is near,   10
But a smile has crossed her quiet face—
    Was someone here?

THE PREHISTORIC HUNTSMAN

They found him deep within an ancient cave
    Bearing the world upon his broken shoulders,
The prehistoric huntsman in his grave,
    Trapped in a crevice by great settling boulders.

In his hand a stone-pick; in his mummied eyes   5
    An eagerness; and pain upon his features
Where the rock-fall caught him with a sad surprise
    And made him one with all earth's humblest creatures.

What did he seek, this wayfarer of old?
    Some arrowed beast crept to its hillside fastness?   10
Or was he bent on dark adventure, bold,
    In alien land, by night's resounding vastness?

Like all his deeds, his very name unknown,
    The vanished mists of time enshroud him, hide him;
Lost in that dim dawn-age he died alone,   15
    Yet all who gaze upon him walk beside him.

WITCHES' SABBATH

The wind is wailing in the willow trees tonight;
    By forest track

The flitting figures gather in the pale moonlight
    For magic black.

While creatures cower in their burrows, silent all,   5
    Strange witch-lights flare,
Demonic revel holds dark, writhing forms in thrall,
    Their wild eyes glare.

Phantasmal fire burns the band of sorcery,
    The bat-things weave,   10
And taloned shapes of evil stalk, for one night free,
    Walpurgis Eve.

FOREST SHAPES

They are curious things that hide in the woods
And cower behind the black tree boles
With their faces dissolved and deathly heads
Where the little lithe worm still tumbles and crawls,
And a rat-like sound of pitter and patter,   5
And the echoing mirth of a sullen mutter,
And the dirge of a wind that whispers and dies
Over the treetops, under the boughs,
While scattered leaves in mildewed heaps
Cover the form whose hand still gropes.   10

THE DREAM THAT DIES

Like a creature unseen as it scurries and passes
With whispering steps through the wildwood grasses,
Like the ghost of an echoing note
From a meadowlark's passionate throat,
Like the rustle of small   5
Blown petals that fall,

Desolate, lonely, and far
As a cindering star,
Like the sound of the sea or the rain,
Murmur of all things that wane,   10
Like foam in a tempest scattered and thinned
Or vanishing leaves that drift off with the wind,
Like a mist that fades into sodden skies
Is the dream as it dies.

THE SLEEPER

The world is an opium-dream;
    I am the sleeper
Who follows an endless stream
    Nightward and deeper.

THE MOON-GLEN ALTAR

She will go in the cold moonlight
    Over the dreaming grass;
To her tryst she will go in the night,
    As the wind she will pass.

Through the still, sleeping glade   5
    Of the woods to a spot forlorn,
She will move through the moveless shade
    Awaiting morn.

She will halt in a secret place
    Where the trees form a little dark room;   10
She will halt where the moonrays trace
    Arabesques on a tomb.

She will sink on the cold, cold ground,
    She will pillow her head

On the old and grass-covered mound   15
　　Where he sleeps with the dead.

There, ringed with dark trees holy,
　　She will rest on the lawn;
She will dream as the night wanes slowly,
　　Till the coming of dawn.   20

Trees solemn and soundless and tall
　　Will watch while she waits on the stone;
But she, in decadent fall,
　　Will wait, alone.

THE MORNING OF A NYMPH

She wakens with the dew yet cool upon her eyelids
　　And softly rises to rejoice in dawn;
She lifts her young faun face to greet the flushing sky, bids
　　Night be gone.

Quiet hangs over all the world; in adoration   5
　　She waits the coming of the golden guest;
A leafy light and shadow-patterned heliation
　　Moulds her breast.

The sun's rim slides above the flaming, far horizon,
　　The radiant god ascends with warmth eternal,   10
And glowing brightlier, awakening seem the skies, on
　　Fire, supernal.

She drinks the earthly and heavenly beauty of morning;
　　She hears the birds' glad rapture and singing glee;
Dawn breaks abroad; then happily she dances, turning   15
　　Toward the sea.

DEATH AND THE TRAVELER: A FRAGMENT

Death: I offer you such dreams
As you have never known;
I offer you the moan
Of Acherontic streams;
I offer you my whole vast Hadean domain   5
For you to reign.

Traveler: I scorn you, Death,
Your rotten breath
Offends my nostrils. Go!
I can not bear you. Go!   10

Death: Turn not, oh Traveler, wait!
The poppies of the dead
Are black and gold and red,
And in their solemn state
My thrones majestical, imperial, and great   15
Await your kingly head.

Traveler: I scorn you, Death.

Death: I offer you the wealth
Of all my timeless lands,
Blue rubies won by stealth   20
Of dwarfs in deep Lethean sands;
I offer you phantasmal gems
More fabulous than all the gems of fame.
Strange wondrous jewels and diadems
With monstrous fires aflame.   25

Traveler: I scorn you Death.

Death: Oh Traveler, these I offer you:
The songs that Sappho sung
And magic garlands flung
By Paphian maids in gardens swallowed of the sea;   30

The lips of Egypt, Troy,
And Aphrodite, every dream you seek;
The vanished joy
Of golden voices that again will speak;
The sound of ancient lutes   35
And silver flutes
That play for pagan festival.
I offer all
The glory of
A thousand and a thousand years ago,   40
All things that you might love,
All things that you would know.

Traveler: I scorn you, Death.

Death: Ah Traveler, scorn me not
          For I will help you find—   45
          Have you forgot?—
          The face that haunts your heart and mind.
          In my domain alone you'll capture
          Your soul's desire, all lasting rapture,
          All past and future. Traveler, stay!   50

Traveler: Not now, not yet. I go my way,
          I still have far to go, it's late.

Death: However far you go, I wait.

Traveler: Goodby, but if we meet again—

Death: We will. We will, and I know when.   55

Traveler: Not soon for I must find a song—

Death: Not long, not long. . . .

Sanctity and Sin

KING OF THE SHADOWLAND

Uncrowned though king I rule alone
    And hear no sound except the sea
    That murmurs dirges soft to me,
That murmurs with a ceaseless moan.

No shadow falls athwart my halls   5
    No echo answers when I speak;
    No light illumes the frieze antique
That slowly crumbles from these walls.

I hear no voice on fading wind,
    I know not what or why I wait;   10
    No more will any pass the gate,
My hosts are gone in eons thinned.

A worm that's feasting in a tomb
    Is lord of more than I, a king,
    Who know what after-time will bring,   15
My world is death, my kingdom doom.

I ponder on the million years
    My race arose and passed away;
    I ponder on the crumbled clay
Wherein lie all my serfs and peers.   20

The waters creep, the waters lave
    The shore whence all but I have fled;
    My kingdom dies, my world is dead,
I rule the shadowland, a grave.

ISHMAEL

I

Crowned thrice with cypress, endless times with laurel,
Blood-brother, boon companion to the yew,
From having watched the dead rose petals strew
Wildly, wildly, round features mandragoral
With mystic earth, thereof for ever choking,
He turns, and now returns to unheard choral
Antistrophes that seven before him knew,
Till thus, from incantation and invoking,
He wins the long awaited separation
Of flesh and spirit, and attains the crown
Of inner ecstasy and exaltation
Desired of many but achieved by few.
To this he gives his only adoration,
The world of which no tale is handed down.

II

Ring upon ring, with stone walls sevenfold deep,
He barricades himself against the world;
From towers topless as the realms of sleep
Where banners of his proud name float unfurled,
He scans the regions lying all around,
Barren or fertile, rich or thin and poor,
Where peasants till starved earth and long dead ground,
Or hunters canter shouting toward the moor.
Each vespertime, he wearies of the view
And slowly paces to an inner hall,
Discovering there an equal leaden hue,
Then wanders onward while the shadows fall,
Until, once more, when mistily comes the morn,
He sees them ride, and hears the ringing horn.

Sanctity and Sin

SONNETS OF THE MIDNIGHT HOURS

After Sleep

It is not blessed sleep. It looms as hateful,
As dreaded as some strange disease's pain,
As fearful as the haunts of the insane.
The days for which the heart should be most grateful
Are sick with memories awesome, eerie, fateful,   5
Of nights that seemed eternities, of vain
Attempts to flee from depths where hope was slain;
Of secret worlds that have no name or place.

For in the midnight hours, when sleep descends,
I dream through realms where naught begins or ends,   10
Where all things are, yet are not; time and space
But phantoms; life and death part each of other;
Where far, unhuman beings' dark embrace
Holds me till in unending dooms I smother.

Purple

There where I wandered, purple shadows ran
Across a purple ground to purple cliffs
And back; and purple suns flamed northerly
Across a velvet sky. And when I came,
And when I crossed the imperial weaving span   5
Of purple leagues, violet hippogriffs
With wings of beating purple flew to me
Through sullen skies empurpled with vast flame.
And so I soared on pinions of the night
Through mightier gulfs where still the purple rule   10
Held sway, with purple dreamlands all around.
And when my steed permitted me to light,
I seemed to sink in some huge cosmic pool,
And in a sea of purple shadows drowned.

The Old Companions

Amidst great cobwebs hanging everywhere
My old companions waited all around:
Stray hands and heads that crawled; in nests I found
Part human creatures creeping from their lair.
Out of a dusky corner came the stare   5
Of some gray form that made a rattling sound.
Along the walls dwelt living mummies, bound
In swathes of softly searching sentient hair.

What goal, what new companion did I seek?
Was it an hour? Eternity? A week?—   10
Until I felt that tongue or talon stroke
My neck, and heard that husky, gurgling choke
As of some ancient corpse about to speak. . . .
I could not move though mind and spirit broke.

The Head

The head most strangely seemed like one I knew;
It rolled, and spun, and stopped in front of me,
While its pale eyes kept watching patiently
Till memory slowly came, and knowledge grew,
It was my own; my own face showed that hue,   5
My own the lineaments that seemed to be
Bloodless, the blind eyes of eternity,
The mouth where something dark was trickling through.

It watched me, waiting, while I stared as long
As all the years of Hercules' great labors,   10
Stared at my own dead eyes unearthly lit.
Oh heart, cease beating; eyes, close; sight, be wrong:
The head sprang high; but slashed by unseen sabers
It fell in parts, and I was part of it.

In the Attic

Slowly I climbed the worn old attic stairs
In darkness absolute, and listening hard,

For what, I did not know, yet tense, on guard
As I went onward toward those upper lairs.
Then at the top I stood on magic squares   5
That glowed with fitful lights, and each one starred
With signs unreadable, on each the shard
Of some imprisoned thing with old despairs.

I watched them till, from out the greater dark,
The swart hand crawled, through mid-air lengthening,   10
And I drew back, but still the hand with stark,
Tremendous fingers, growing, strengthening,
Pursued and pounced; an arm that had no source
Yet twined around me with inhuman force.

The Cocoon

My loved one made soft cooing sounds, and so
I stroked the glistening webwork on its head,
The strange cocoon, not living yet nor dead
But inbetween; whose phosphorescent glow
And shining eyes bespoke caresses, slow   5
And languid, warming into life; no dread
Had I, although I knew on what it fed,
The substance of it in the long ago.

But all at once the shell of that cocoon
Burst; mindless, mewing as it tried to speak,   10
Not woman, man, or child crawled in my lap,
But something from the dark side of the moon
Whose black, scaled body had for head a beak,
A beak that, darting, closed me in its trap.

The Metal God

In that far, future time where I was fleeing
Through mighty chambers, hunted and alone,
I came upon a curious great throne
Where sat an even greater, stranger being,
A king who saw but used no eyes for seeing,   5

A metal titan shapen like a cone,
Quicksilver, pulsing with a deep soft tone
That filled all worlds, all space; vibrations freeing
All substances and creatures from the bond
Of aimless life, of aimless death. Long since   10
The hands that wrought it vanished in its power,
And I, though struggling, in that selfsame hour
Felt flesh dissolve in motes of silver tints
That streamed to join the nothingness beyond.

The Little Creature

Oh little creature, lost in time and space,
You've come again. You keep me company here,
You drift upon the moonlight hovering near
And watch, or seem to watch, me for your face
I can not find, nor do I seem to place   5
Your limbs, if limbs you have; nor is it clear
What form you have, for always you appear
Changing and new, so hard to know, to trace.

Oh little creature, whether old or young,
Make this your home for I will make it yours;   10
And though you never talk (do you have tongue?)
I'll talk of future times and alien shores.
Oh little creature, here's a tale of doom. . . .
How strange. How strangely empty is the room.

The Pool

Unto my feet a little trickle crept
Progressed slowly underneath the door
And widening inch by inch along the floor
Until, my shaking limbs grown weak, I stepped
Aside. The flow turned toward me, and it kept   5
Increasing, spreading more and ever more
As if there never were an end in store.
Now here, now there I fled; still on it swept.

Around me, solid walls of no escape,
Before me, one closed portal, and the flow   10
Whose source could only be some fearful shape
With blood that had so curious a glow;
The door must open, showing why the hue
Of this fresh pool of thin and brilliant blue.

The Prey

Vast wings were flapping in the night. I heard
Them fill the air with measureless strong beat—
What nameless hunter searching for its meat?
So huge the wings, I wondered what the bird
That clove through midnight where no other stirred,   5
What sight in later hours would haply greet
The dawn, when those great wings had made retreat;
For in the talons I was fast immured.

Though endlessly we traversed far abysses,
At length all motion ceased, upon a crag.   10
And when the talons loosened, I could see
The burning harpy eyes, head of a hag,
Before I dropped away, for I was free—
To fall amid colossal precipices.

The Torturers

As I remember, there were clanging gongs
That beat the air to frenzy; dirges, knells,
A tolling like a myriad decibels
From metal monsters humming voiceless songs.
As I remember, there were flaming tongs   5
That flayed my flesh, and I was bound by spells
Of lunar sorcerers; a thousand hells
Were better than their hideous, measured wrongs.

As I remember, in my agony
I begged the gods to save me from such pain.   10
I heard a sound of cosmic revelry,

Then beating to the chambers of my brain
The answer came, where I in torment lay,
For silence unto silence died away.

The Statues

I knocked upon the portal till with clang
On long, metallic clang, the brazen door
Curled inward, flowerwise. I stood before
Weird, lifeless birds that talked and harshly sang.
Quick to my side two black, sleek leopards sprang   5
With eyes of golden fury; while a score
Of revelers turned statue, and no more
Their mirthless muttering through the palace rang.

Past them the leopards led me on and on
Where vast, dark marbles stood in endless miles,   10
And when I saw these titans, thereupon
Their enigmatic laughter filled the aisles;
But when I passed and left them in their gloom,
The vacant halls were quiet as a tomb.

The Hungry Flowers

The fleshly flowers whispered avidly:
This being's face is soft, he shall not pass;
And all the little jeweled blades of grass
Made mutterings that sounded like low glee.
I looked across the great plain warily.   5
Those glittering swords that shone like splintered glass,
Though singly impotent, might be in mass
A savage, indestructible enemy.

So hesitantly, I put forth my foot
To seek, beneath the flower-heads, a path.   10
I found my leg become a hellish root,
I saw the hungry flowers toward me crawl
With bright-eyed ecstasy, exultant wrath,
And on my flesh their mouths, devouring, fall.

The Hungry Flowers

The Eye

A deep force pulls me toward the window-blind,
Some impulse urges me to raise the shade;
Why is it that I tremble, half afraid,
With formless terrors running through my mind?
What are the dim dread images that bind   5
My hand? Why is my arm so strongly stayed?
What sense of overhanging doom has made
Me fearful? What the sight that I shall find?

Some warning voice calls out: *Go back—go back!*
I could not turn though fronted by the rack.   10
And so I slowly raise the shade to greet
Whatever on the other side should lie,
And stare and stare in horror as I meet
The leering of a huge and sightless eye.

The Rack

They clamped hot irons on my throbbing head;
They poured fresh acid on my blinding eyes;
They added madness to my frantic cries
By bathing me in streams of molten lead.
They slit me till a hundred new wounds bled;   5
They burned me, bound me with deep-knotted ties;
They crushed me, broke me till I could not rise,
Then hurled me, shapeless, on a needle-bed.

Beyond the rack's red searing agony
One thought more torturing usurped my brain,   10
A thought my tongueless mouth could never speak;
Though they, with cruel joy, had given me
This never ending night of mounting pain,
It merely hinted of the coming week.

Sanctity and Sin

Escape

Now was I destined after all to die,
I who had fought so hard to reach my goal?
Would maggots in my starved, gaunt body loll
When I collapsed beneath that burning sky?
The sun stared on me like a blood-red eye,   5
In all this hideous land the only soul.
Yet, when toward farther desolate wastes I stole,
I thought ironic laughter passed me by.

Though they who tortured me were far behind,
My bloodprints in the dead sand marked my trail.   10
Each step eternal, on I struggled, trying
To reach the haven I would never find.
I stumbled onward, knowing I must fail,
For they were deathless hunters, I the dying.

Capture

They caught me in the wasteland in the west,
Caught me with safety but a league away.
For my escape I knew what I must pay:
Tortures would mark the finish of my quest.
They dragged me back with never pause for rest,   5
Back through the desert for those fiends to flay,
To burn, to break; their pleasure not to slay
But punish, since their power I dared to test.

The dark, walled city slowly came in view,
The magic towers, the skyward thrusting spires,   10
The windows burning bright with eldritch fires;
And when at last my captors bore me through
The ebony gates, one savage curse I cried,
And I, and all that phantom city, died.

In the Pit

Now they have buried me in this dark pit,
And all around their other victims wait,
Like me uncertain of their final fate
Though they are broken too, and their flesh slit.
There's one small shape that mews upon a spit;   5
The chewed remains of something used for bait;
Another mass their hungry pet half-ate,
Rejected. Nameless others near me sit.

They gave me back my eyes so I could peer
Around and see the comrades that are mine;   10
They left me morsels, curious and queer,
To make my sufferings worse if I should dine.
I know that I'll by them be watched for ever
And in recurring deaths escape them never.

The Unknown Color

Whence came that unknown color? Was its source
Beyond the violet, within the red?
Impalpable, a brain-shaped thing of dread,
A glowing form, it drifted on a course
Malefic, purposive, with alien force   5
That followed through the chamber where I fled.
I found no door, and when all hope lay dead
I tried to scream but heard no sound, no hoarse,
Despairing cry. I crouched against the wall
In that dark chamber, numb with terror, mute,   10
Nowhere to flee, however I might strive,
The unknown color hostile in pursuit
That swiftly toward me now began to fall,
A sentient entity from hell, *alive.*

Monstrous Form

I saw from that dim cave where I was hiding
Atop a mountain measurelessly high
That pierced the blackness of a starless sky

Sheer cliff and rockfall miles below. There, sliding
Across the rubble, creeping, crawling, gliding,   5
A monstrous form surged on and searched with cry
As of a lost and hungry child. Then die
I must, for it arose, its mass dividing
To limbs alive with wormlike, writhing fur,
And stood tremendous to my caverned room,   10
A giant shape part human, part despair,
The face a group of eyes above a blur
From which a tongue curled inward to my lair,
Engirt, and hurled me nightward into doom.

Nightmare in Green

And after this, there came to me one green
    With all the dreadful cerements of the grave
    Who shambled down the midnight's empty pave
With flapping tatters and long talons lean.
And of its face no vestige could be seen,   5
    And of its flesh the rotten remnants gave
    No hint of what it once resembled, save
That force demonic brought its eyes their sheen.
And of that thing swept over me a fear
    So great I turned and clawed my hands to bone   10
        To flee, but where I crawled, wherever fled,
And everywhere I looked, I saw it near,
    Its footsteps shuffling closer on the stone,
        For I was its, that horror from the dead.

What Followed Me?

What followed me across the lifeless plain?
    What shape of evil? What its foul intent?
    I struggled onward though my strength was spent
And every forward step a weary strain.
And still it followed, still I heard it gain   5
    Until I stumbled. Fear no longer lent
    Me hope. I fell, though flesh itself be rent
And I in all that solitude lie slain.

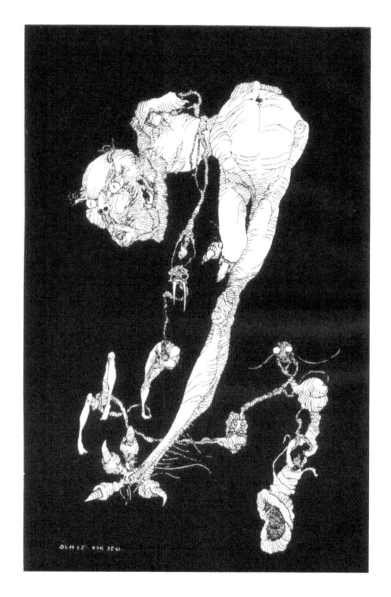

What Followed Me?

I saw it then, two trunks that fused as one,
    The rooted feet that walked with measured stride,   10
        The branching arms that reached with taloned tips,
And burning eyes along each limb. It spun
    One fleshy tentacle, raised me beside
        It lifted toward its dark, devouring lips.

Fantastic Sculpture

Fantastic shapes and forms loomed everywhere
Throughout the sculptors' workshop, uncomplete
Save one upon a dais standing tall,
The naked torso of a goddess glowing
Rose-pink, and outward thrusting from each bare   5
Breast tip a vine; the striding legs for feet
Had hooves, the arms no hands but splaying fall
Of creepers, and where head should be was growing
A tuft of slender tentacles, a crest
Of blue-red veins erect, a spiral swarm.   10
I turned on stealthy step lest something hear me,
Then came the rush of hoofbeats and, soft-pressed
Behind, the thirsting tips upon me, warm,
That nightmare sculpture, running fast, was near me. . . .

The Tree

In silence absolute the lifeless land
Stretched farther than horizons. I could see
No moving thing, no blade of grass. One tree
Alone protruded from the desert sand,
Its branches leafless, yet a budding hand
Stood out, half-open pods showed mystery   5
Of human form or beast, weird sorcery
Of bird and fish in nodules like a band
Of knotty burls along the trunk, and clung
To every branch. The tree had long since died,
But all the strange and withered things still hung   10
Upon it nevermore to leave. I tried
But could not move or even draw one breath:
I too was fastened on that tree of death.

The Bell

All night I heard the tolling of a bell;
All night I heard the cadences of doom
Across the boiling seas' own muffled boom;
From sunken cities rose the solemn knell.
The waters mounted in one surge whose swell   5
Laid bare the mystery of the vast sea-tomb,
And from those giant caverns' lifted gloom
The tolling came like measures for a spell.

Then all the seas united with a roar
Of wave that smote against colossal wave,   10
Engulfed again the riddles of the ocean;
The bell beneath the seas, beyond the shore,
Grew fainter in the silence of its grave;
I heard alone the surging tides in motion.

The Ultimate Vision

I dreamed the waters of the world had died,
The ocean beds were open now, and free,
And all strange things once covered by the sea
Showed everywhere, while flopping creatures died.
There lay a bed of shells and bones; I spied   5
A city of a vast antiquity;
Ten thousand ships and more; shapes great and wee
And weird encrusted forms on every side.

I saw the vales and mountains of the deep,
I saw the dwellers of the ocean night,   10
The weedy pastures and the drowned, the dead;
And in the fading vision of my sleep
I saw rise up a substance soft and white
That feebly moved its pulpy, eyeless head.

SOMEWHERE PAST ISPAHAN

Now I am bored with all things brief and transitory,
With love, and life, and death, and even with ennui;
Now no things interest me,
And I am sick alike of passion and of glory,
Of days and nights that are an old and tiring story,   5
And dreams that can not be.

Weary of all desires grown monotonous,
I sink back in the pillows of my deep divan
With the lithe Persian,
And indolently languish in her languorous   10
Caresses, though I find slight joy in amorous
Delights of Ispahan.

Great wealth have I, a kingdom own, with palaces for pleasure,
Jades exquisite, delicately carved ivory,
And polished ebony,   15
And lissome houris, gems and gold in many a measure,
But what is there in wealth? In treasure what but treasure?
Things of small worth to me.

I turn away from diamonds, rubies, emeralds, pearls,
I find no surcease in the unrelieving wine;   20
I clap, and at the sign
Come forth my slaves and eunuchs and the dancing girls;
I hear the music's plaintive sob, watch spins and whirls.
But ennui still is mine.

Burn incense till the fragrant air is odorous,   25
Till jasmine, oleander, or full roses' bloom
Quite overscents the room,
And drowsyhead gives way to dreams more slumberous,
And weary drag of minutes grows less dolorous,
And life less like a tomb.   30

Bring hashish, cannabis, or sleepy opium,
And of the empty dreams that were not worth desiring,
When of this pastime tiring,
O Cyrenaya, take away the sweet, dark gum,
Unclothe you, scent you with nard, myrrh, olibanum,   35
Make you fair for admiring.

Dance, Cyrenaya, while I watch you swaying slowly,
The green-flecked amber of your smoky-lidded eyes,
And if you mesmerize
Me from my ennui with your body naked wholly,   40
And sinuous, then I will raise you from the lowly
To love's sad paradise.

And if you charm me not, and I grow weary of
The kohl that shades your eyes, your breasts with henna tipped,
And your mouth poppy-lipped,   45
And if your kisses, like most kisses, mean not love,
Rubies I yet will place in that jet hair above
Your body slender-hipped.

But I grow weary of your sensuous caresses,
And of your lush young beauty I grow wearier   50
Though none is lovelier
Than you. I have drained all delights from long impresses
Of your bright lips, all pleasure that your flesh possesses,
And all love's joys that were.

Now I am bored with all things present, all things olden, 55
And melancholy, dream away the afternoon
That scarcely passes soon
Enough, while drowsy minutes lengthen to hours golden,
And dream caravans of Nirvana are beholden,
And houris sad songs croon.   60

I only find more ennui in philosophies,
Doubt everything, doubt that I doubt, and wearily
With all things disagree,

Or quite agree—it's all the same; no virtues please
Me, and I sicken with the languid unsurcease   65
Of earthly ecstasy.

I know that nothing is worth while, all things are quite
Futile, futility as well; that all things wane,
All pleasure and all pain,
All substances and dreams, all sorrow, all delight,   70
All present, past, and future worlds; and day, and night;
All lacking, and all gain.

So muse I while the endless, aimless minutes wear
Away, and listless hours voluptuously flaunting
Remembered raptures haunting   75
My withered heart, stained as with vermeil and rich vair,
Till evetide falls, and the Muezzin call to prayer
The faithful, with far chaunting.

And *La Illaha illa Allah! M'hamed rasul*
Allah! the kneeling figures in devotion pray,   80
Till softly falls away
Bismillah wa Allahu Akbar! when with facile
Grace, true believers, with burnouses flowing gracile,
Withdraw till dawn comes gray.

Now day dies, and night falls, and that great summer moon   85
Floats up, and bathes the burning air still shimmering,
And the cicadas sing,
And champak fragrance makes the drowsy senses swoon,
Enchantment grows in this soft after-nightfall noon,
And fair seems everything.   90

From somewhere in the distance voices fall and swell,
And faintly comes the echo of a traveler's song,
Of caravans that throng
The roads to distant marts; and Allah's blessed foretell
Rich ends, and soft the tinkle of a camel's bell   95
Begins the journey long.

Into the moonlight, Cyrenaya, I would go
And leave behind me all the weary works of man,
And take the caravan
To heart's desire that only I and Allah know,   100
The outer-lands where all's a dream, and dream-winds blow
Somewhere past Ispahan.

UNCOLLECTED POEMS

THE POET'S LAMENT

I am telling you goodbye, dear,
And I hope that you won't cry dear,
If I never take you anywhere again;
Though I know that you are pretty,
That your words are clever, witty,   5
You have never been inspiring to my pen.

If your name were only Mabel
Can't you see that I'd be able
Quite to make it match in verse most anytime;
But alas! Your name is Myrtle,   10
And it only rhymes with turtle. . . . . .
I could never love a girl with such a rhyme!

THERE WAS A SMELL OF DANDELIONS

(A parody on Quarterly poetry)
[with Hjalmar Bjornson]

We listened to the strange rain
Falling on the window-pane
Tall candles there were dreaming
By the luscious curtains gleaming.
Strange songs filled the air   5
From the one reciting there.
Poems ripe, red, rich, and rare,
Like a steak half roasted there.
We listened to these strange tall dreams
On which the cool green rain gleams.   10
And a smell of dandelions was
Over all the tall wet grass.

THE CLASSICIST

[with "P. V."]

Oh what a classicist am I,
Agricola, agricolae.

I know all Latin stems and nouns,
The names of all the Roman towns;
The authors' names I know by rote,   5
And any Latin phrase can quote,
And to the students in my classes,
I'm quite as good as ears to asses;
And in my greatest bliss I am
When I can make my students Cram.   10

Agricolae, Agricolarum,
Or any other words to jar 'em;
Comparisons and conjugations,
And philological relations,
And other such-like things as that is   15
I offer to my students gratis,
For they are life and love to me,
Bright jewels on the knowledge tree.

Oh what a classicist am I,
Agricola, agricolae.   20

Illussimae and classicorum
Are things that never ought to bore 'em.
They also ought to know their Caesar,
Or else they're much more dumb than geese are.

And when I die, must be enscrolled   25
Upon my tomb, this legend bold:
"Oh hail to thee, and et to Brute;
He surely was a classic beauty."

Oh what a classicist am I.
Agricola, agricolae.   30

PEDAGOGUES

They blandly sit upon their stools
And think the words they drop are jewels.
Instead, they sound like Major Hooples
That murmur to their sad-eyed pupils.
They're always right, they can't be wrong,   5
The coeds only get along
And win the prof's eternal pity,
Especially when their knees are pretty.
The pedants utter strange conceits
To prove the brilliance of their wits,   10
Quote scholars dead in Alfred's time,
Who knew why Romans didn't rhyme,
Expound a learned fourth dimension
Peopled with ghosts of their invention,
Exhume forgotten platitudes   15
To illustrate their attitudes,
Still live a hundred years ago,
And wonder what we're coming to.
In their ideal, idyllic college,
The janitors would drip with knowledge,   20
The very mice absorb their wisdom,
And learn the use of "ge" and "isdem."
And in this pedagogic cloister,
Each pedagogue, a happy oyster,
Within the limits of his nose,   25
Would rant and dream and drowse and doze.
And perfect students, all in rhythm,
Would chant their perfect lessons with 'm.
And every prof, a second Firkins,
Would be as old as papa Perkins,   30
A model professorial wonder,
Say, sixty-five, not one day under,
For who could ever be a prof.
Who plainly wasn't old enough?
If this were done to Minnesota,   35

Why, there each young M.A. would go to,
For surely none would think of spurning
Such dazzling stores of useless learning!
And Mr. Briggs would watch their English,
And every error, he would single-ish!   40

STREET SCENE . . .

"Miss Shere, are you a kind person?"

"I beg your pardon, I don't know you."

"I'm asking you, Miss Shere. Are you a cruel person?"

"Certainly not."

"Saturday night then, Miss Shere. What time?"   5

"What are you talking about?"

"Us, you and me. What matters except us?"

"A great deal matters. Who are you?"

"Ely Forchamer, Miss Shere. I'm white and virtuous and fairly goo—"

"Tut-tut, Mr. Forchamer. You're not. You're homely."   10

"Huh. Well, maybe. But I'm sociable, Miss—"

"You're offensive. That's what you are."

"But I'm perfectly moral."

"Masher. Disgusting."

"Well, I guess I'll be going. I'll be seeing you."   15

"You certainly will."

"But Miss Shere—"

"Nine o'clock Saturday night, Mr. Forchamer."

CHANT TO THE DEAD

Blessed be the dead for they are dead.
Blessed be the living for they will be dead.
Blessed be the unborn for they shall be dead.

THE SCHOOL OF SEDUCTION

Archibald Mimmih ran a neat
    School to teach seduction;
With each lesson came complete
    Personal instruction.

The school was more than popular   5
    With scholastic ladies,
Who came from near and came from far
    And asked to go to Hades.

To forty thousand species, Woman
    Mobbed him to induce him;   10
Goddess or devil or only human,
    They paid him to seduce 'em!

POEMS FROM BROKEN MIRRORS

Fling Wide the Roses

Fling wide the roses, ere the petals all be faded,
    Drink deep the cup, ere thou canst drink no more;
Live riotously, ere thy life for death be traded,
    Love, ere thy lips dead lips alone adore.

Sing, for too soon, too long, thy mouth shall know no singing,   5
    Take, or the taking never will be thine;
And when thy surfeit comes, then die! and die a-flinging
    Red roses in the overflowing wine.

Drink!

Drink! For you'll soon have the earth for a cover!
　　Drink! For the joy of the winking wine!
Drink! For the red-stained lips of your lover!
　　Drink! For the night and the fruit of the vine!

Drink! For the pleasure, forget sad thinking!　　　　　　　5
　　Drink! For the flagon is full and deep!
Drink! For the sheer great joy of drinking!
　　Drink! Till you fall in your wine-full sleep!

The Dead Mistress

The maid I love was buried long ago;
　　The dust of centuries lies on her head;
　　Nothing remains of her; her ancient bed
Is only known in realms where dream-winds blow.
Her eyes are blind; her sweet white limbs but know　　　5
　　The endless silence of the endless dead;
　　A thousand and a thousand years have fled;
She has been swallowed in the years' long flow.

No voice remains to tell me where she lies,
　　There is no picture of the dear dead face,　　　　　　10
　　　　I know not whether she was slave or queen;
Or if, beneath those warmer, clearer skies,
　　She had a lover for her wondrous grace;
　　　　I only know she died in Mytilene.

My Lady Hath Two Lovely Lips

My lady hath two lovely lips,
　　Made for love, made for kissing;
Who can blame the mouth that sips
　　Such a treasure? I'd be missing
Joys that pass and youth too fleet,　　　　　　　　　　5
　　Springtide waning, Beauty sweet,
If I thus forgot to meet
　　Duty, in her lips caressing!

Aftermath

I have awakened in the fevered midnight noon,
    In the breathless rapture of the scented dreamful air;
I am the night and the garden and all things swoon
In the mystical burning pallor of the moon
    Shimmering everywhere.   5

I walk in the steps where the Beloved and I held tryst;
    The hot, still air is sweet with heavy perfumes;
By the breath of its shameless lips I am lightly kissed
Where, drowsy and drunken and dreaming, nod and list
    The summer blooms.   10

Why do I shrink from the soft red mouths of roses
    That tremble and shiver with passions that lately were?
A venomous, waiting, and phallic orchid dozes,
A tiger-lily opens and fails and closes
    Dreaming of Her.   15

Wonder and beauty and terror are hanging all over,
    The garden is still with a fever that passes all name;
The monstrous spell of the night is an amorous cover
For the soft flowers awaiting the lips of the lover
    With a sweet rapture of shame.   20

Delirium over my shaken soul now passes,
    A nameless and sorcerous glory has made me weak;
For something unknown in the flamingly riotous masses
Of flowers and marvellous jasper and coral grasses
    I vainly seek.   25

The Beloved is gone; I known not the way she has taken;
    I am blind in the white embrace of the moon's hot stream;
I find no rest in the passions with which I am shaken,
The night grows dim and unreal and reeling: do I waken
    Or only sleep?   30

Credo

Life is a dream between two deaths; a blind
Unmeaning march from nothingness to night,
Wherein sweet terms, as Love, and Hope, and God,
Are merely words that mean no more than life.
All things are symbols of eternal death—   5
The ruined relics of the ancient past,
The dying wonder of the world that is,
The soon-to-be-forgotten future days.
All nature whispers but her one word: Death.
The trees, the birds, the fleeting springs, the years,   10
The mountains and the rivers whisper: Death.
A million million men have lived and passed,
And found, the one reality is Death.
A million million men will live and pass,
And find, the one reality is Death.   15
The sum of all man knows, the sum of all
The years since Time began, the sum of thought,
The sum of hope and faith and life, the sum
Of all the stars and all the universe,
And all that ever will be known, is Death.   20

IN MANDRIKOR

They dwell in dying Mandrikor
     Where livid lichens freak the plain,
     And faint stars fret the dead skies pain,
And all is mute forevermore.

They dwell in wasteland and in night.   5
     And no thing else abideth there
     Save only they who everywhere
Are crowned nocturnal lords of fright.

For many a thousand leagues about
     Terrific things hold fearful sway   10

That war eternally on day
And change the name of Night to Rout.

And all is dark, and all is still,
    And underneath the chuckling gloom
      Awaits a nameless ghastly doom   15
Whose sight hath made the great Death chill.

No traveller ever crossed the land,
    And none will prove its monstrous Fear,
      Or pass the twining things that rear
From out dark forest, bog, and sand.   20

Upon that distant evil star
    They hold in mirth their mad domain,
      And antique wizards try in vain
To slay the fiends in magic war.

SONNETS OF THE MIDNIGHT HOURS

Dream-Horror

Now they have buried me in this dark pit,
    And all around, the weary corpses lie;
      They know that it will take me years to die,
Although my flesh with many knives is slit.
They would not burn me quickly on their spit;   5
    How much more exquisite to hear me cry
      With only rotting corpses lying by,
And bloated carrion rats that near me sit!

They left to me my eyes, so I could stare
    Around, and see the comrades that I had;   10
They left me also rotten corpses there
    To keep me company lest I go mad;
And then they left me, lonely, lying where
    The worms with endless, spoiling flesh are glad.

The Grip of Evil Dreams

There were great cobwebs hanging everywhere,
    And awful things were lying all around—
    Wan hands and heads that had no trace of wound,
Foul nightmare creatures peering through the air;
And from a dusky corner came the stare   5
       Of some white form that made a rattling sound;
       And there were living, ancient mummies bound
In gummy cloths of long and human hair.

These charnel horrors made me sick and weak,
And yet I could not move. There came a creak,   10
       And then I felt a tongue or talon stroke
       My neck, and heard a husky gurgling choke
As of a yellow corpse about to speak. . . .
       How glad I was that I at last awoke!

The Creatures

Vast wings were flapping in the still night air;
       I saw great shadows across a gibbous moon;
       The mandrakes moaned along the black lagoon,
And in the sky, there hung a baleful glare.
Terror and death seemed stalking everywhere,   5
       And still those vast wings beat that sullen tune;
       Were they strange creatures from Outside that soon
Would seize their prey and seek their cosmic lair?

Out of the night, there came a shrill long scream,
       And through the riven air, there harshly swept   10
       The charnel sounds of awful slaughtering.
At first I deemed it some mad nightmare-dream,
       But from the sundered room I never crept—
       My face was eaten by a red, huge *Thing*.

The Red Specter

There was a red, raw dripping thing that mowed
    And tottered in a spreading pool of blood;
    There was a shape, on which a scarlet flood
Enwrapped it in a steaming blood-red shroud;
There was a sound, gigantically loud,   5
    That seemed to pour from where the horror stood;
    There was a crackle as of blazing wood,
And all the air was misty as a cloud.

And both my hands were covered with that red,
    And everything was red and strange and mad;   10
    I scarce could know the evil that I did;
The air from some vast stellar carnage bled
    And veiled the shrieking shape in haze that had
    Red phantoms in its bleeding mystery hid.

Doom

Oblivion had laid its deathless curse
    Upon all things of life and time and space;
    Of death itself, there now was left no trace,
And DOOM had fallen on the universe.
The heavens like a dead, colossal hearse   5
    Contained no thought or dust of thing or race;
    In all infinity was left no place
Where Death in death all things did not immerse.

For Death the Conqueror at last was king;
    His realms were vacua, he proved his vow   10
    That all would pass, that nothing would abide.
Not anywhere was life nor anything,
    Nor vestige of the worlds of old; and now,
    Upon his fallen kingdoms, God had died.

MOON MAGIC

The Glow

O Love, a flower closes
    Upon the crimson eve,
    And wood-winds lightly grieve
      For sunlit earth;
Deeply the folded roses   5
    Dream of forgetful day,
    Sleep the dim night away
      For dawn's rebirth.

Grown faint, the winds drift slowly
    Over the jeweled grass,   10
    And footsteps seem to pass
      Where none are seen;
And flowers fair as moly
    Rise in the pale starlight,
    And voices shake the night   15
      Until, between

The worlds of sleep and waking,
    All things their form reveal,
    And dreams become the real.
      The real world dreams,   20
With magic murmurs making
    A music in the air,
    And fair things yet more fair,
      Till Nature teems

With wonder past all knowing,   25
    And beauty yet unknown,
    And light that never shone
      On fields of noon,
And every dream-form glowing
    With refluence of flame   30
    Stranger than ever came
      From any moon.

O Love, my world is pouring
    Its voice in one vast song
      Wherein a cloudlike throng   35
        Of phantoms move;
O Love, my heart adoring
    The image and the fanes
      Where nothing else remains,
        Binds you, O Love.   40

The Song

Out of the well of the heart and the heart's recesses
Comes love, and all the beauty that love possesses,
A glow that develops and flows from the inner being
And illumines with mystical light the eyes unseeing.

I am awed, O Love, at knowing this mystery,   5
I am awed that the moon and stars are so close to me,
I am awed that flower and forest and leaf be shaken
With ghostly winds that whisper to them, Awaken.

O Love, the world so shadowy and dim
Murmurs the music of a magic hymn;   10
Is it the glow so magically bringing
To birth the song that all the spheres are singing?

So luminous, O Love, the shrine so holy,
So soft the sound that stirs the night so slowly;
It is the blessing of a Druid's prayer,   15
So faint the dream, O Love, and yet so fair.

The Overtone

A flame of the stars, Beloved, burns out of the far-flung spaces
    Leaving the night more luminous than light of the moon;
A wind from worlds beyond blows out of foreign places
    Rippling the leaves that sleep in a moonless midnight noon.

Your eyes, Beloved, are filled with the beauty of strange stars glowing   5
    In splendor of birth and dawning there where the worlds begin;

A wind from the spheres that through your shadowy hair is blowing
  Moves from worlds without to enchanted worlds within.

It is so strange, Beloved, that everything has blended
  To make the unison of this half-heard overtone;   10
It is the ceaseless song that love began; unended,
  Unending, a tale, even to him who tells, unknown.

The Dream

We are one with the stars, Beloved, and witnessed the young sun's dawning
  When light shone out of the mystical ebb and flow;
We were present when space grew heavy with seeds of its own spawning,
  And oblivion saw strange worlds begin to glow.

We have lived through cycles of birth and change, through cosmic ages,   5
  We have dwelt with new suns and watched the old stars die;
We have read inscrutable symbols on dim, dynastic pages,
  We have been participant and passer-by.

From the dust of forgotten worlds to whole new systems leaping
  To birth, we have witnessed the past and present blend;   10
We have seen in the future time, and space, and the universe creeping
  With weary steps to the old, original end.

We are deathless, O Love, and deific; we have known the wonder supernal;
  We have been the dreamed-of, the dreamer, the fugitive dream;
We have found that only the dream is unchanging, O Love, and eternal,   15
  That nothing exists but the vision, the thought supreme.

DEAD FRUIT OF THE FUGITIVE YEARS

The Dream Changes

I know there are no princesses, but you
  A princess are, with beauty lovelier
  Than any known in lands that never were,
When Nielsen with a pen of magic drew

Phantasmal realms of faëry, strange and new,   5
    Where moons are high, and only dream-winds stir,
    And young Prince Charming rides in quest of her
Whom spells will fetter sleeping till the true
Love comes. I know that I shall never be
    He who may lift the spell, and yet I seem   10
    Content to know the image of the dream,
A music-maker, lord of sorcery,
    Chaunting of moon-dim princesses whose clime
    Is dreamland, out of Space and out of Time.

Surrender

These are the things I love you for: the gray
    Green eyes you hide yourself behind; your face
    So lovely with its skin so fair; the grace
That's natural artifice in you; the way
You move; the unexpected things you say;   5
    Your hair's soft brown or gold; your hands that trace
    Slow patterns in the air; the warm embrace
Of lips too tender; your precise array.
These things I love, yet words can never tell
    The subtle pleasure that you give to me,   10
    The inner beauty I more deeply care
For, and the loveliness you watch so well.
    Oh love, it is enough that I may be
    With you, and you so beautiful and fair.

Though All My Days

Though all my days were added one by one,
Like cardinal numbers adding without end;
Though every day were filled with benison
Of sleepy hours that time and plenty send;
Though every hour were rich with a great store   5
Of beauty's rarest harvests, and the hours
Differed so, each from each, and this one more
Than that just passed held sweeter, fuller dowers;
Though this were Paradise, and Paradise

Radiant and ever-freshening, ever new,   10
Yet would it be no Eden to entice,
Nor I desire it if it held not you;
And I would let it in complete eclipse
For you, or for one kiss from your soft lips.

The Second Beauty

You are the fairest of the lovely whom
        Beauty possesses, but I would not care
        How fair you were, if you were only fair,
If in your head or heart, there were not room
For beauty of the mind, where, as on a loom   5
        The spinning threads weave patterns rich and rare,
        Thought fashions worlds that earth can never share,
Else beauty were as lifeless as a tomb.
I love you for the charm earth gave to you,
        For things external, but of higher worth,   10
I love you for the realms of endless view,
        The lands no traveller ever found on earth;
I love you for the beauty all can see,
And more for beauty only known to me.

Twice Excellent Perfection

Your moods are dear to me, and all the ways
You care for that warm house of all your own,
Its superficial vesture whose arrays
Reveal the symmetry that should be shown
To all the world; and dearer still are those   5
Arrays and disarrays the house contains,
The changing fancy and the careful rows
Of modes that will not match despite your pains.
Your imperfections are as fair to me
As your more supernatal beauty, since   10
Perfection gains by contrast and may be
Twice excellent; thus your slight flaws evince
The artistry external, and I find
Delight in sudden vagaries of your mind.

This Larger Room

There is a room, Beloved, that you'll inherit,
And through its darkened window see no sky;
There will be none with you to help you share it,
And you will never know what years drift by.
And it may be that you will find it lonely,   5
And it may be that you will find it fair;
And it may be that you will find it only
An emptiness not knowing you are there.

Now wherefor do you make this larger room
A counterpart of what is still to be?   10
Are these bright ways foredue to that one whom
You will become? It seems so strange to me
That you make these to that a sacrifice,
And all your days, and mine, a vain device.

The Woman Answers

Surely this beauty was not meant for keeping
        Encysted from the sight of other eyes;
        Surely the loveliness that men say lies
In this sweet earthly house was not for sleeping
The years away intended, but for leaping   5
        To brilliant flame, whose splendors mesmerize,
        Then blind, the favored ones; while I, more wise
Than they, sow seeds for harvests of no reaping.

I come to men with unrequiting passion,
        And should a mouth as pleasureful as mine   10
        Yield grace to only one, deny the rest?
I answer—if they love me in my fashion,
        For I give love like sips of precious wine
        To those that bless, and by my charm, are blessed.

The Deadly Calm

My life-illusion has at last been broken,
        And I look on with clearer, colder eyes,

Remember phrases with a vague surprise
That I confused the words you'd plainly spoken.
You proved illusion not more strong than oaken   5
    Planks riddled through by worms, that he is wise
    Who finds impersonal and calm the skies;
My mind, not heart, is now my soul's true token.

I am not sorry to have been your lover,
    For you have taught a thousand things to me,   10
        The deadly hardness of reality,
And truths I could not otherwise discover.
    Romantic dreams, illusions, poetry,
        Were errors that have lost their hold on me.

Corroding Acids

I am a fool, for only fools would trust
    Your polished phrases spoken carefully,
And overlook the underlying thrust,
    Or think that those sweet words were meant to be
What they appeared. But there are some so blind   5
    From love or faith or trust—fools—who believe
What they are told, the falseness never find
    Till acids of experience undeceive
Them, and the words so beautiful and sweet
    Assume new meaning and become the prick   10
Of daggers, fair appearances retreat
    And naked lay the true design, the trick.
The acids would not matter, nor I rue
Their ravage, if they had not come from you.

With Cat-like Tread

The fall of footsteps light and pantherine
Came near me, passed, and faintly died away;
And of my presence, I could feel no sign
Of recognition, nor was I to stay
The chance, the pattern, call it as one will,   5
That says, *These things shall be,* and they are so;

I merely listened, as I listen still,
And waited, wondered, though I did not know . . .

I have met darker nights than that of old,
Felt deeper silence broken by no sound,   10
Heard legends not by earthly voices told,
And only echo answer a low call.
I listen, but I do not hear them fall,
The footsteps pantherine upon the ground.

LYRICS OF DOUBT

A Testament of Desertion

Why am I sad?
For the winds that have blown,
And the days that are dead,
For the springs that are gone,
Thus am I sad.   5

Why am I weary?
For the times that are over,
For the grain that is reaped
And the fallen sweet clover,
Thus am I weary.   10

Why am I old?
From the fury of living,
And a bitter full heart,
Deep loving, dark thinking,
Thus am I old.   15

What do I want?
Nothing of farthest or nearest,
Nothing of future or present,
Only you, and the past, my dearest,
This do I want.   20

To the God of My Fathers

I bow beneath this fruitless unattaining,
    Doubting, I stumble blindly to thy feet,
    And for thy wine, than earthly wine more sweet,
And for thy bread, than my bread more sustaining,
        I seek through chambers of thy strange abode;   5
No hope, no faith, no fear, no trust remaining
    In that bare wall where my fists wildly beat,
    I come, weary yet bearing still this load.

I ask no comfort and no ease of thee,
    Nor that thou roll away the mountain boulders   10
        And point out ways to rapturous rebirth;
Nor that thou give my sightless eyes to see,
    Nor lift a burden from my crumpled shoulders;
        I ask for blankness and the dark, dark earth.

MARMORA

Out of the west, foul breezes sweep,
Out of the dark where the black moons creep,
With the breath of the web-faced things asleep
    In Marmora.

A ruby flares in the glistening sky,   5
In the marble palace, gold dwarfs cry,
Long-dead creatures murmur and sigh
    In Marmora.

In a marsh that even the water-snakes spurn,
Mandrakes writhe and witch-fires burn,   10
Swart talons toward the ruby turn,
    In Marmora.

All night the blood-red ruby glares,
Before the palace a beacon flares,

But the spell-bound half-beasts lie in their lairs   15
         In Marmora.

Out of the sky, a black star shines,
From the palace, a marble monster whines,
On the throne a king for its worm-queen pines
         In Marmora.   20

Smooth is the liquid ink of the lake,
On its shore, mad emeralds burn in the brake,
A slain man moans on a pointed stake
         In Marmora.

THE CYPRESS-BOG

Lethal waters sleep and swoon
By a cypress-veiled lagoon.
Flickering flames and fire-flies
Burn beneath the stagnant skies,
Lighting swamps and tarns unholy   5
Where miasmal stenches slowly
Rise from half-decaying logs
And the miles of rotten bogs.
Sucking sounds invade the night,
Air and water creatures fight.   10
Shrieking, thus to settle whose
That dead body in the ooze.
Footprints of a man-bat woven
With the fresher tracks of cloven
Feet are ended in a fen—   15
Neither thing will walk again.

THE MONSTER GODS

The monster gods wait in the heart of the mountains,
The monster gods dream an apocalyptic dream;
The monster gods sleep by Faëry's phantom fountains,
The monster gods hide where the fen-fires gleam.

The elder gods have promised a day of returning   5
When post-historic revels will unfetter them,
When skies turn to flame in a universe burning,
And ashes consume what the elder gods condemn.

The monster gods then will tremble and waken
And rub out the granules of sleep in their eyes,   10
When death has been captured and time overtaken,
The monster gods will answer the Ancient Ones and rise.

The monster gods will walk then from hills and from highlands,
When four-dimensioned vaults revolve and open wide;
They will spew from the sea and climb from sunken islands,   15
From time-gulfs and planes of space they will glide.

The monster gods wait in the heart of the mountains,
The monster gods dream an apocalyptic dream,
They sleep a long sleep by Faëry's phantom fountains,
And they hide in eerie lands where the fen-fires gleam.   20

A QUEEN IN OTHER SKIES

Her queer, ensorcelled eyes
        Are like the secret pools of Jupiter,
                Concealed with opalescent mist whose fall
And rise
        Is as the fall and rise of mist of myrrh.   5

So deeply dark and fair
      Behind the amber lids they dimly dream,
            Imbedded witches' jewels mystical,
Whose rare
      And violet depths with flameful passions gleam.   10

Her eyes of eidotrope,
      Mysterious as her sunken palace is,
            Are languorous with dreams of mighty doom,
And ope
      To ponder old, unsated malices.   15

Discoverlessly far,
      She rules a realm decayed from elder days,
            An empress regnant in an empty tomb—
A star
      Beyond the black beyond the stellar maze.   20

EPITAPH TO A LADY

She liked the texture of a lily,
      The sight of goblets cool and rounded,
The thought of Wilde in Piccadilly,
      And scandal, better if unfounded.

She liked to don herself in raiment   5
      More modish than the current mode;
She often made the first down payment,
      And for the rest, she owed, and owed.

She loved no man, so she would boast,
      No human being could be near her;   10
She loved alone and loved she most
      Her own reflection in a mirror.

She loved to play a dangerous game
        So long as there was never danger;
And lovers, fat ones, old ones, came   15
        And steadily grew strange and stranger.

Her latest lover's love was such
        That she had always invitations,
For she paid half, when they went Dutch,
        And paid for all, on some occasions.   20

The primrose path she rarely took
        Because she sometimes fell or stumbled;
Forsaken often, she forsook
        The lanes where hopeful virgins tumbled.

A paragon, except in virtue,   25
        A beauty, save in soul and body,
She claimed that thoughts, not deeds, pervert you—
        Her thoughts and deeds alike were shoddy.

She hated all lies, save her own,
        Believed no truth except what pleased her;   30
She reaped the whirlwind she had sown,
        Yet saw no cause why gossip seized her.

Her laugh was like a silver bell,
        Devoid of mirth, devoid of feeling;
Her gestures supplemented well   35
        Her vestures; both were quite revealing.

With her sweet self, she had no quarrels,
        She said she lacked experience;
She had no scruples and no morals,
        And thus preserved her innocence.   40

PORTRAIT OF A LADY DURING A HALF HOUR WAIT WHILE SHE FINISHED DRESSING

This is the Wedgwood she lifted, the saki she quaffed, her
Lips parting and closing over the draught her
Fingers raised; there hangs her mirror—poor mirror—
That saw her but heard neither her voice nor her laughter.

There stand her books, the Willy Pogany Alice   5
In Wonderland; Rothenstein's portraits done with malice
Not too malicious; the strangeness of Harry Clarke's Poe;
And Machen to read when she thinks of the fabulous chalice.

The flagons and bottles and jars that cover her dresser
Stand waiting to perfume and powder and softly caress her,   10
Elizabeth Arden, Walska, and Rubenstein;
She is new each time that their contents grow lesser, and lesser.

A single gardenia lies with delicate grace in
The midst of her things; a girdle, as though to chasten
Heretical eyes is casually hung on a chair;   15
The essence of her is here—but I wish she would hasten!

THE LITTLE GODS WAIT

The little gods wait in the heart of the mountains,
    The little gods dream an apocalyptic dream;
The little gods sleep by faëry's phantom fountains,
    The little gods hide where the fen-fires gleam.

Their elders have promised them a day of returning,   5
    When post-historic revels will unfetter them,
When skies turn to flame in a universe burning,
    And ashes consume what the elders condemn.

The little gods then will tremble and waken
    And rub out the granules of sleep from their eyes;   10
When death has been captured and time overtaken,
    The little gods will answer their elders and rise.

The little gods will walk from hill and from highlands,
    And four-dimension vaults revolve and open wide;
They will spew from the sea and climb from sunken islands,   15
    From time-gulfs and planes of space they will glide.

The little gods wait in the heart of the mountains,
    The little gods dream their apocalyptic dream;
They sleep a long sleep by faëry's phantom fountains,
    And they hide in eerie lands where the fen-fires gleam.   20

[POEMS FROM *INVISIBLE SUN*]

I am as mad as mad can be,
Nothing on earth can bother me,
Great big moonfaced politicians,
The cat on the fence, and world conditions,
Emily Post, and thieves in state;   5
Working hard for pieces-of-eight,
Finding that life from end to end
Means ditched by your girl and left by your friend,
None of these things can bother me
For I am as mad as mad can be.   10

Dig and delve
Till a quarter of twelve,
Then away, away,
It's the break of day,
Or twilight's fall   5
Which is better than all,

Sanctity and Sin

And you and I
Alone know why,
So dig and delve,
It's a quarter of twelve,   10
Away, away.

There was a young woman I know
Who liked it above or below,
In front or behind,
And she didn't mind,
There always was farther to go.   5

[LIMERICK]

There was a young man—such a pity!—
Who burped a remarkable ditty,
    Till with derrick they capped him,
    Ran a pipe-line that tapped him,
And drew gas for the whole of Sauk City!

ELEGY

Farewell, good friend. You leave us now. And yet,
    As you begin your final travel, know
That we who linger here will not forget, can not forget
    How greatly you have guided us. We go
        Ennobled by your grace, your love—beside you,   5
        Returning humbly our own love whose force,
Joining your journey, brings our living light to hold you, guide you.
        Only do we who knew you feel the source,
    Enriching us, of your own everlasting glow.

SEPTEMBER HILL

Here on the hillside by the great gnarled boughs
Of oak the leaves fall in autumnal haze
While over us the wind at twilight soughs,
And past the winding river's end you gaze,
Resting beneath the shadow curtain falling   5
Down the far closure of the valley, sky,
Earth and eternity. Is some voice calling?
Whose whisper in the quiet darkness? Why
And how and whence the steadfastness, the source?
Now in the mind come messages unspoken,   10
Drifting as leaves but urgent with a force
Restoring all things lost and small things broken.
Evening to night, and night to afterglow,
I take the bridgeway you already know.

I AM MAN

I am man.
I am the master of each living thing,
I am the hunstman of each fleeing kind,
I am the arrow of the cosmic mind,
I am wisdom of my own self blind,   5
I am man,
Of man I sing.
I am builder, I am maker,
Greater than
The great Creator,   10
I am my own final taker,
I am man.
I am slayer, I am slain,
I am fire,
I am sod,   15
I aspire
To play God,

Sanctity and Sin

I am the empty brain
Of man I tire.
I am sunlight on the hill,   20
I am mist in midnight hollow,
I am doom that all dooms follow,
I am foam torn free of storm waves cresting,
I am dust in cosmic outways resting,
I am mote   25
As I note
I am man.
I am all cups that fill,
I am the fleeting dew,
I am all deaths that chill,   30
I am all life that springs anew,
I am man.
I am sower, I am reaper,
I am wastrel, never keeper,
I am seeker,   35
Never finder,
Briefer, weaker,
Longer, blinder
From the riddle of the rib
As from birth   40
While I pass by
I rule the earth
From the cry
Of infant in the crib
Till I end   45
As I began,
Random child
Running wild
Round the bend,
I am man.   50
I am instant lost in time,
I am atom lost in space,
I am the triumph of all-seeing eye,
I am the cinder wiped away,
I am night erasing day,   55

I am nothing as I die,
I am man.
Who knows when I first began?
But when my span
In aeons closes   60
As the unknown force disposes
Building on to what goal later,
What end smaller
Or much greater,
Not on earth nor anywhere   65
Will atom keep
In endless deep
Or starfire care
Of right or wrong,
Of why the plan   70
Or know the song
That once was man.

GOLDEN POPPY

The legend saith: for each, the golden poppy blooms
But once, for every soul in mosque, at sea, on sand
Of unknown timeless land;
Now I, at dusk, beside the wall of ancient tombs,
Have seen the golden poppy spread its petals fair   5
Where none could know or share.

The legend saith: for each, nepenthe follows sorrow,
And past Nirvana waits eternal vision, pure,
Past golden poppy's lure,
Past where, once seen, once open, close in no tomorrow,   10
The golden poppy glows in beauty with the light
Of black and radiant night.

The legend saith: when each lone traveller passes by,
However brief or stilled, or borne on farther turn,
The golden petals burn,   15
The golden poppy folds and each eternal I
Becomes that single soul, the unity beholden
To poppy legend olden.

The legend saith: wherefor does any legend matter?
The true believer makes his own faith all along   20
His life, his love, his song;
And though all poppy seeds in final chaos scatter,
The golden poppy once again will grow to bloom
And night's great arch illume.

SOLITARY

I hear them in the grass when I am walking
        Along the summit island lanes of shrubs and trees;
I hear them when no human voice is talking
        On bridges, river trails, on every gentle breeze.

I hear them in the rubble of defaced land   5
        In heat of summer day or cold of winter snow;
I hear them in the meadows and in wasteland,
        Deserted city streets, and fog, and lantern glow.

I hear them wide awake or part way resting,
        I hear them over thunder, and at midnight gloom;   10
I hear them when I am not even questing
        In all the silences that haunt a vacant room.

I hear them in the spring rise and in fall ways,
        I hear them by the lake shore and at cliffs of stone;
I hear them in the open and in hallways,   15
        And listen always as I journey on alone.

LINES

Here at the house you dwelled
    In love bespoken,
Here, by the hand you held
    In bond unbroken,
All the least lines that spelled   5
    For you were token.

POEMS IN PROSE

THE ONE WHO DIED

Years ago, I died. They say I live, but I live not; I died long years ago. In what age or cycle of my existence, I can not tell, for I do not know. The passing years in their vast, accumulative procession have erased the memory of that time; I know I died, in an aeon lost amid the inconceivable antiquity of the abyss in its dawn; I know this, but I know only this. What day—what year— what cycle I can not tell; I have forgotten during the immemorial cycles that have since elapsed. The day is buried deep in those vanished ages which marked the birth and death of stars, the waxing and waning of universes, the rise and dissolution of the cosmic throng; the day is lost amid the changing succession of abyssal night and abyssal star-illuminated splendor; the day is forgotten in the flow of the sands of eld, in the ebb-tides of time, in the mists that lie upon the long, unmeasured ages and the ancient aeons scattered along its path through the dying abyss. That year, I say, is beyond memory, beyond recollection; the scrolls of Space and Time have no record of it; there is no trace amid the lost ages, and the lost cycles, and the universes which have come and gone, leaving no memory in the ever changing deep.

We were together then; you, deathless, and I, unknown of that change to which all save we are thrall. We were together, in our alien sphere where none but we could enter; timeless and spaceless and remote we dwelt in our mystic realm. We took no heed of the phantasmal universe, of the ephemeral stars, of the spectral birth and death of visible things whose duration was scrolled in dust. We were aloof from the shadowy and impalpable existence wherein dwelt the peoples of oblivion; we alone existed from the dawn of time, and we alone passed, eternal and deathless, through all the ages and all the cosmic mutation and change that swept civilizations and worlds into nothingness, and whirled universes out of the night and back to the night. We had met, in the strange glory of chaos and far realms unknown of others; we had met, in the mysterious labyrinths of night where stellar chorus answered planetary song in radiance and gloom, in white flame and ebony; we had met, pursuing celestial trails through the distant, unexplored throngs of stars and suns.

We had met, then, and we had loved; I, as one who knew many mysteries and sought all knowledge, and now found one mystery transcendent; you, as one who desired, but owned neither limit nor mastery. Vainly I sought and vainly I questioned. In that old epoch, when we two were there in all our alien supremacy exploring the trackless infinite, watching the ebb and flow of star and starflame, I questioned. Mutely and silently I waited the reply, thoughts surging up within me even as the stars surged in our often precipitate quest. But slowly and passionlessly came the response. And I listened while the mute stars stared from all around, and turned toward the spaceward flowing windows of night, and into the measureless and labyrinthine abyss I followed again the unknown trail that lost itself among the stars, vaguely and vainly seeking solution of cosmic mysteries.

THE MESSENGERS

Long have I searched in Time and Space, but they are gone. And long have I travelled to that land, but it is barren.

I had passed beyond the Western Portal, on that day of old, far, far beyond, and now had come to a desert. Upon the horizon a dying sun forever sank but set never, and its red rays crossed the forbidding sand to illume the ruined fanes of a people who have vanished and are forgotten. And standing there, I looked about. The dull and sombre sky was watching them, and them, too, I watched as they travelled. They came, I know not whence, and passed, I know not whither, phantoms that thronged across the heaven mutely. None other eye but mine could see, and none other know that they have come and gone. All day I watched them pass, the Messengers. What wonders did I see! What splendour! What fabulous riches in that silent-wending caravan! Perhaps they were the offering of some ultra-stellar king, richer than the richest dream, who wooed the stately, marmoreal queen of Polaris; or the spoils of an interplanetary war raging unquenchable among the Titans of star and star; or the tribute of a captive world sent to the conqueror across the deep. Illumined by the rays of the westering sun, the envoys and their burthen passed—richly figured tapestries, gold, and green, and purple, stuffs woven by the velvet-fingered artisans of Aura; great jewels—emeralds, and rubies, and opals, and precious gems never known to man; rare perfumes gathered from the flower that blooms only in the inaccessible vales of Aldebaran; strangely carven ebony; slaves, and queer beasts, and indescribable priceless things from emperors and planets of the remoter infinite. And their passing was like the richly figured tapestry, or like pageantry of the gods.

Often have I wandered in that desert; and often, now, I stand and wait. But the fires of the dying sun have cooled and become ashen in the long years that have passed, and the dusking skies brood darker. I wander disconsolate in the ever shifting sands of the desert, while the ruined fanes are

Sanctity and Sin

swallowed in the rapid-running sands of time, and the wind whispers lonely across the ancient desert, and the dunes creep and flow as I vainly wait.

For the Messengers have passed.

THE PURSUERS

In the bloody glow of sunset they came, all hideous in its red rays, while I cowered back watching them. Under the dying twilight in a rapid ghastly rush, they swept across the smouldering sky, fiendish with their alien, malefic hate. Beside them sped unleashed quivering things that sought the ancient trail of the Messengers. Prophetic was the portent of that silent passing in the dull, burning sky, a portent of cosmic evil sent abroad. In the fascination of fear, I watched the monsters rush by, monsters the tongue affords no terms to describe, beasts whose name would sicken horror, loathsome, loathly entities that tore adown the dim-felt trail in fury. And there were some I could not see, that could not be seen, but the air thickened where they travelled, and the shapes were indescribable. In trailing line they journeyed, but they journeyed on the wings of light, an avenging hurricane that stormed after the fugitives. Out of the depths of space they came, and into the darkling deep they rode. The air itself brooded at the phantom passing, and the immemorial desert waited, desolate, for the usurpers of the sky to vanish. But for long hours, the horrid throng hastened on its way, with malevolent faces ablaze and bloody under the bleeding sky. And through all those long hours, I watched the pursuers rush from the unknown and depart, threading the trail among the trackless stellar labyrinth beyond. The lurid eye of the sun stared at them from low upon the western horizon; in the dreary waste of desert and the smoking sky, all that moved was the horde which swept across the heavens.

They are gone, out of the glowing sky into rayless night, questing still the far, stately parade of the Messengers. The sun is lower on the dim horizon, and the empty vault is bleak. And now the cosmic drama is veiled forever.

PAPHOS

This is immortal Sappho, old as the deathless Greek who sang the deathless Greek of old; this is fabled Helen, young as the fable of Helen and for ever walking the world anew; this is amorous Aphrodite, queen in the Hellenic dawn, and queen across the ages. Long ago, she, deathless woman, worship of love and lover and loved, walked in Mytilene, and Athens, and Cnidos; to her they built a temple in Paphos where fabulous roses bloomed, and the poppies were red as the blood red wine, and eternally young as she, eternally young, and queen, and loved. Hers was the rapture of winged youth, and the worship of maidens with vine leaves in loosened hair and myrtle on brow, dancing naked in the golden dawn; hers was the glory of fair, forgotten faces, burning in the bright sunshine; and hers the offering of cupped breasts of the maidens of Lesbos. They brought her Hyblan honey to soothe the honied lips that ruled in Paphos; they brought her nectar and ambrosia, her, sweeter than nectar and ambrosia, sweeter than all the costly profferings of youth and maiden; they brought her juice of the crushed grape, to stain with purple lips more red than the reddest rose and darker than poppy bloom; they brought her purple wine from the warm vineyards of the south, and crystal water from the crystal springs of the gods. At twilight, Pan piped across the hills, and reedy notes floated on the wind to the temple of Aphrodite, and wild melodies from the pagan piper drifted down the hillsides calling maenad and centaur and satyr, while the trembling maidens waited. And light fingers plucked the strings of lute that answered lute and chorus calling to Pan invisible, and immortal songs sweetened the scented night. And pattering of hooves sounded on the turf of spring, and faint noises came out of the dark, where dancing satyr claimed dancing girl, and body to naked body was clasped, and youth claimed youth in golden rapture. The restless centaurs leaped amid the olive trees, and sought shy maidens, trembling in the twilight. The seilenoi came in search of fresh nymphs, beautiful and unguarded. Pan piped closer, and charmed away the dancing feet of girls that followed in rapture the rapturous melody. And the maidens flung garlands of violet and wild rose from their brows and loosed their streaming tresses to the warm winds of the sea and the south, and lifted high the purple juice of the grape and drank to the purple night. They flung the cups away, and abandoned themselves to night and the joys of night. Strange fruits were picked for the midnight feast; the half-gods brought lotus and luscious sweets, and red and purple wines for the revel. This was Sappho, this was Phryne, this was Helen and Aphrodite, queen of the ages and queen of the beautiful and queen of love and lover and loved. Dark was her temple at midnight, but the fires burned in the woods, and the forms of maenad and centaur dancing passed and repassed while satyrs leaped to claim the frightened maids that fled. These were the feverish embraces, these the hot breaths of satyr that panted for young girl and seilenos that sought assuaging of his lust. Dionysus was king of the revel, Aphrodite queen of the revellers; the crushed grape was the food of maiden and semi-god, and the tables were laden with fruits and things that grow in the fields; but the grape and the wreath and the red red rose were king of the feast and the feaster. The amorous girls wore sacred violets in their tresses and strewed wild roses before the hooves of the centaurs, and lightly danced away from pursuers with flushed faces luring the half-gods, and white skins and warm, white breasts gleaming in the dark. Eros was great in the dawn of love, Aphrodite was great in the dawn of beauty, Helen was great in the dawn of woman, Sappho was great in the dawn of love and beauty and woman; but the wine god ruled, and Eros was lord, and the two walked free in the night of spring, the praise of maid and centaur and queen; and the one was great, and the other was great, and the revellers sang the praise of both to the wild, wild pipes of Pan. All night, the wine god ruled, and Eros ruled, and the forest was dark, and dark the bower where centaur and mae-nad, maid and satyr lived and loved in the night of spring in Paphos. The roses scented the warm night air, the violets grew in bower and glade, the fabulous poppies of Paphos budded and bloomed; the maidens wove garlands of the flowers and put wreaths on their brows; the maidens wove violets in their hair and strewed petals to the winds and the night and the great gods Pan, and Dionysus, and Aphrodite. O night of old and maiden of old! Greece was great in the youth of the world, when love and beauty were one and all, when the gods walked on the fertile hills, when the wine was sweet and spring was sweet, and Pan piped songs of birth and rapture, of youth and beauty that never grew old, and love that never had end. This was the glory of Greece. This was the glory of Paphos. This was the glory of the queen Aphrodite, praise of maid and praise of youth and praise of love and lover and loved.

THE WOMAN AT THE WINDOW

The sun had bled for ages over that strange land; old and dying it was now, but still it bled, even as it swung down the final path of its history. The land had grown old with the aging sun; and now it too was exhausted and deso-late where it stretched away for long distances under that lurid orb.

A tower rose from out the midst of the land, a tower old and crumbling, a tower of curious architecture and fantastic lines. No man knew when it had been built. It was born with the land, and with the land it was passing away. But it rose yet, in the middle of the red kingdom, and the sun as it sank each evening looked back for an instant on the castle, tall and ancient, that stood amidst the timeless realm. Sinister it was, as it rose, lone and terrible, in the ghastly rays of the sun; more sinister it was, in the utter desolation and solitude of the land wherein it lay; and yet more sinister it was, with its ruined walls crumbling, and its stones falling away, and the red sun coloring it with evil shadows in the day and dreadful shadows at twilight. In the dead night, the castle dreamed in darkness, for the seven moons of old had long ago disappeared into the black void of the starless sky. But at dawn, and during the day, and at twilight, the castle was a visible and evil landmark arising like a mute sentinel or an exiled ghoul out of the level lands around it that stretched far away. In ages, the land had known the touch of no feet. In aeons, not a creature, not a being had broken the silence. Never a step was heard on the sands that wasted away in the desert. Never a sound disturbed the solitude of that horrible realm. Only the castle rose, mute, ghastly, and eternal, bathed in the red of the one huge deathless sun; and its wall crumbled, and the grains fell, but it stood yet, infinitely old and weary.

There was one great window facing the west in the tower, a queerly shaped window with fantastic traceries and odd arabesques figuring its surface. There was none other in all the castle save this one grotesque opening that faced the west. It was a dim entrance to the unknown interior, an obscure and antique opening which alone gave ingress. Every night, the sun paused for a moment on the horizon, and its fixed, staring eye peered across the red waste to the castle that rose like a crimson horror. For a minute at twilight the blood sun paused, and the fantastic pane colored and smouldered and glowed with ineffable evil fires, and curious crimsons ran across its surface until it lighted up wildly as if the interior burst into spectral witchfire. Dull red was the sky; crimson the sun; the land was old and of a reddish hue; and the castle itself a scarlet spectre at dawn, and a crimson sentinel at day, and a blood-red age-old fiend at twilight with its one red-illuminated window staring at the staring sun.

And when the window began to glow at twilight, and the scarlet rays swept across its surface and turned it into a sheet of blazing red, a strange transparency crept into it, and the window dripping intangible blood limned with a hellish indistinctness the face of a woman peering out. Her eyes were fixed on the motionless sun; in the minute at dusk when it halted, and all the strange land was a study in reds and shades of red, and the sky itself the color of liver and the realm livid with blood red rot in its length and breadth, the face became visible at the window while curious and exceptional rays left the sun and turned the window into fire. But no illumination ever reached the face of the woman who stared, and at the end of the twilight moment, when the crimson fire duskened on the pane, her countenance slowly disappeared into the mysterious and phantasmal gloom that filled the interior.

For, even as the sun sent livid waves across the window, her face became visible, motionless and gazing into the west; but eternally dark and indistinguishable though the scarlet rays made efforts to illumine and outline it; and when the baffled sun retreated, the face of the woman at the window was reclaimed again by the guardian shadows that came from the remote recesses of the castle.

It had always been thus. In the youth of the crimson realm when the sun blazed in the bright red of its dawn, the castle had stood, and the woman had peered westward at twilight. In the maturity of the land, when darker colors had erased the orange reds of youth, her face appeared still at eve, unfathomable and shadowed and eternally staring at the spectral sun. And now, in the old age of the immemorial realm, when its cycle was running to its end and the reds were all dark as old blood save for a moment at sunset when the window burned with ruddy scarlet, her countenance still was outlined for a minute, symbol of a mystery that not even the worn out sun could solve. No one ever left the castle. No one ever entered. It was timeless as the realm, and changeless save for the slow corruption of age, and fixed as the many and singular shades of red that were a part of the land. And no one knew whether the woman ever left the window, for she was motionless when the twilight rays outlined her face and motionless when they retreated to the sun.

And now the lurid sun was approaching extinction, and the land no longer lay under hot and painful crimsons but slumbered with suffocating dull reds and dark blood-colors filling the heavens and oppressing the castle and the antique realms that stretched around it. And at twilight, the sun still labored with futile efforts to send its last livid rays into the castle, while the window smouldered and glowed redly. And even yet, the woman at the window became visible, peering with ceaseless and unfathomable scrutiny at the sun, eternally watching, eternally waiting. When the sun was near its final eclipse, her face was still behind the red window, staring westward. When Time lay heavy on the realm and elder prophecies of Doom were nearing fulfillment, her mysterious face even as long peered from the window. And when Night descended on the realm and obscured forever the castle and the window and the sun and all the curious and abominable and insane reds, the rays at twilight left the sun for the last time and colored the window once again with the last glow of that frightful color which dominated the entire land.

And the woman at the window was staring at the staring sun.

EBONY AND SILVER

With a little shiver, he entered the palace that bathed in a cold flood of moonlight. When inside he listened for a moment in the dark and marble halls. And, hearing no sound as the echo of his entrance died only in hollow ricochet, he crossed the hall. Coming on a door, he pulled and slowly walked through the great marble room. In it stood a marble statue as black as ebon, a statue of Venus, cold and coldly beautiful. A silver frost was on the room so that silver lay upon the black marble floor and silver on the marble Venus. Slowly the man walked to the Venus, with his naked body silver in the light and his shadow lengthening in silver and sable over the ebony marble floor. By the statue he paused, and with silver on the statue and silver on the floor, he stood straight in motionless waiting. The ebony Venus on its pedestal was cold and marmoreal, the chill face, polished breasts and body gleaming in black and silver, cold as the tomb. He who entered looked upon the naked Venus, black marble in a vast, black marble palace. Within the room all was still. The moon waned westward and the shadows in the room changed as the silver changed in the cold moonlight. But there came no sound from the rigid figure by the statue, and nothing else was in the empty marble hall save the man and statue. The room resolved itself into a study of black and silver. And when his lengthening shadow reached a certain point, and the silver was paler on the black floor and the smooth, black Venus, the man turned, and left the room. Behind him, a glistening marble Venus stood in the middle of a desolate chamber; and silver mingled with the ebony, so that the entire hall was a strange unison of black and silver shadows.

But the hall into which the man passed was neither silver nor sable. It was empty, like the other, save for the statue of a Venus. But the statue was white and delicately modelled, and golden light streamed in upon the statue and the flushed marble of the floor and the walls. And the man walked up to the lovely statue and looked at the softly curving body, whereon the light lay in warm curls. Hesitantly, he touched the exquisitely moulded thighs, and then withdrew his hand and stood immobile by the statue. He made no further motion. He watched the figure while soft light fell upon it and turned the air to golden haze, and brought out the beauty of the white and pink marble floor. The hours waned. He stood yet by the statue, his body and the Venus making a harmony in the room of light and golden shadows. And when the lengthening shadows reached a certain point and the light was fading on the white marble Venus, the man turned and left the room.

Sanctity and Sin

The searchers found him later. They found him lying in the room of silver and sable shadows, lying cold and still. He was groping toward the black marble Venus, and all the chamber was a curious pattern in black and silver, while the shadows were lengthening along the marble floor.

THE DEATH OF THE FLOWERS

There was a secret garden, whose flowers were rare and of a strange beauty. They were as no other flowers. They were many hued and lovely, and of colors which had never before tinted the petals of the blooms of earth. Some of them were fragile, pale lilies whose whiteness was unearthly and spectral and deathly beautiful, lilies of suave grace like maidens cloistered and pure; some of them were roses, white, and crimson, and black, and the black roses were magnificent beyond dreams and beautiful as a witch; some of them were poppies, but poppies of a rich, dark red whose very color oppressed one like a suffocating tapestry; and some of them were orchids of brilliant hue, orchids that flamed with gold and purple and orange and black, orchids whose petals were silken and marvelously beautiful, orchids where color ran riot and the petals were splashed with flame and passion, orchids of surpassing loveliness. There were other flowers, too, flowers of curious shape and ineffable suggestion, flowers that were as symbols of glory and evil; some were poisonously green, and grew straight and alone; and some were of a sinister red; but here and there was one of brilliant orange or of bright gold; and all were rare, and all were delicate, and all from hot lands, and over the garden hung the heavy perfumes of the many and magnificent flowers that made the garden a mass of color and a riot of beauty. At dawn and at dusk, when the flowers opened or closed, the scent of each was separate before it blended with the others, and some were sweet and others were drowsy, and there were some that went to the head like wine, and some that told of far-off things, of beauty and dreams, and strange, dim lands. But when the perfumes blended together in the hot noontide and hung heavy over the garden, they were as a sweet and cloying drug that dulls the senses into forgetfulness.

A tall and stately woman ruled over the garden, a woman whose beauty matched the beauty of the flowers, and her grace, their grace. She was a queen, walking with grave and slow steps into the garden every day to watch the flowers. Her hands were slender and tapering, and her long fingers caressed and played with the flowers with a sort of silken delight. She was beautiful to look upon, but she never smiled. She walked always with languor, and her gestures were slow and listless. And she sat in the garden and dreamed away the scented hours while the sun rose in the glory of dawn, and westered in the hot noontide, and sank in the drowsy twilight. And she held the blooms of the strangest and most exotic flowers in her hands, and the soft petals with their vivid and odd and sensuous colors lay in her palms like the fevered faces of girls in rapture. And the perfumes arose, exquisite and delicate, to her face. But she never smiled. She visited the garden every day, and her mysterious, heavy-lidded eyes gazed on the flowers as if she would absorb their beauty. Not a vestige of decay did she permit in the garden. She found it and she kept it a thing of surpassing beauty, whose flowers had all the colors of the world, solid tones, the tints of every jewel, shades and curious freakings and contrasts which oversplashed the varied flowers with the most subtle and most haunting colors. The flowers never drooped, save with weariness of beauty and overpowering sweetness in the hot noontide; and the petals never fell, save when the tired blooms closed at dusk.

The years were alike in the garden, where the flowers for ever dreamed. The blooms with their insufferable colors and magnificent golds and purples waked and drooped and waked again, and the perfumes ascended to the glare in the heavens, and sometimes hung over the garden in the burning moonlight of summer. And the woman caressed the flowers and sat in her garden, dreaming of mystery and ecstasy while her slender fingers held the feverish heads of evil and beautiful flowers. And the years were alike even as the days were similar in the garden whose intoxicating and perfect beauty lived on in the delicate and fragile and voluptuous flowers.

But one day, the woman did not come. The spoiled petals waited all day, and the flowers in their surpassing beauty and infinite weariness drooped in the glare of the sun, and the soft and brightly spotted orchids closed their petals of poisonous and intoxicating color and perfume. All that day, the woman did not enter the garden. She never came again, leaving, as she entered, in mystery. And one by one, the flowers drooped, and the petals fell to the ground. Foreign growths entered and stifled the flowers, and all the soft and lovely blooms decayed. And in the ruinous garden, the dried stems remained as the only vestige of a surpassing beauty, for the petals were blown and scattered; the lilies, the poppies, the roses, the strange and morbidly beautiful orchids withered to dust and dreams. And with the death of the flowers, the garden even as quickly passed into its sere autumn, desolate and forgotten.

THE PURPLE LAND

In the midst of an immense and silent desert stood a tablet which was perpetually concealed by the purple shadows that dominated all the realm. Forever and forever the desert extended in all directions, yet found no change in the limitless expanse, not in the dead sands, nor in the level sweep, nor in the soundless quiet, nor even in the purple shadows themselves. In the day shone no star, and never a sun or a moon rose to break the enchanted spell; but always, the heavens had been luminously purple, and the stagnant air duskily velvet, and even the vast desert dark and purple like a tapestry under a purple dome. In the elder epochs of times past, the sky and the desert may have been violet; but the succession of years had watched a slow darkening of all the realms as if, like a great fading lamp, it approached extinction. Perhaps, too, in other years of the immemorial land, there had been eyes to watch its purple beauty; but now only one figure walked abroad.

He was swathed in purple robes like a spectre; his face was concealed in purple veils; when he walked, the folds of his robe streamed out behind him in long tatters. Once in great intervals, he came and stood beside the tablet and read it; for it was graven with runes and symbols of a mysterious, antique tongue, and told a strange tale of purple shadows; and there were many differences in the runes as if many different hands had inscribed the legend; and the symbols at the top were so faded and worn that they were scarcely legible. And when he had read this tale of memory, as silently as he came he turned and walked into the purple shadows until the streaming purple tatters of his robe were swallowed in the vast and soundless grave of night and the desert. And each time when he departed, there was one more symbol carven deep in the tablet, as if the history of anterior days were yet incompete, though the face of the tablet was now almost covered.

Then once the stranger walked out of the shadows with his tattered robe flying behind him and read the legend; though now the desert brooded in dark purples of corruption. And it seemed that the heavens and the air were suffocating of purple. And when he turned, he walked slowly and straightly into the immense purple shadows so that his robe did not billow; and far out in the oblivion of the shadows was swallowed. On the sands of the desert was no trace of his steps, nor did he ever return to read the legend.

And on the tablet, the symbols were complete.

THE LOST MOON

Millions of years hence, when oblivion had claimed the old and momentary world of man, there lived upon a strange moon a woman as strange as that abysmal world. For the satellite was lost to the star whence it sprang, and now it spun through the fathomless blacks of night. No ray ever pierced the gloom that overshadowed the moon as it plumbed the stellar deeps. And there was no voice to speak with the woman, for she, and she only, followed the falling world to its unknown destiny out in the cosmic gulfs. She was all of gold, from her hair to her listless feet; and all the curves of her body were heavy with the soft gold whereof her flesh was made. The beings of her race were thus; but they had perished from the desolate moon, and she, the sole survivor of that wondrous land, plunged with her world. Out of the gloom rose many curious relics of that race—vast, fantastic structures, weirdly beautiful palaces and gardens, nameless things that no other moon or world save this had possessed. Yet the woman of gold ignored them all, for she dwelt on a world falling to a mysterious doom, and what avail the relics of the forgotten dead when death is near?

Dreaming of ancient splendor, she lived in a palace that raised symbolic spires to the black sky and its few wan stars. In one room she lived while the moon rushed through spatial abysms; and the room was huge and of a strange metallic substance that glowed as if the black walls, though dead, could watch; and the air, scented with a curious perfume, seemed to have absorbed the death color out of the incense and out of the ghostly-glowing walls so that the woman lay in the pall, weary of oblivious dreams and impending doom, with only her beautiful and magnificent gold body a visible contrast to the black horror of lightless space.

Many days passed, if days they could be called where only unbroken darkness ruled, and where time had ceased to exist. Yet the rapid plunge of the moon was unhalted though it had long left the regions of even the faint stars and now rushed blindly through black vacua which swallowed it deeper and deeper in a mysterious cosmic grave. For now there were no eyes to follow the moon on its strange far course through alien gulfs. A soft heap of gold lay on the floor of a curious castle. And out of the body of gold, with its roots cleaving the marble of the floor, rose a great, gold orchid, whose stem glowed softly, and whose petals were tipped with jet, and whose pulpy center hung wearily and faintly crimson in the night of utter oblivion.

Sanctity and Sin

DREAMING AWAY MY LIFE

Dreaming away my life in dreams of death and beauty, questing forever and questing forever vainly her whom I had loved and lost in the buried days of old, came I, on that lost moon, falling far beyond the utmost universe, to the valley where bloom the flowers of death. Then came I there, to that strange realm where passionless eternal flowers dream a passionless eternal dream of death. And lo, the flowers rise beside a silent pool of ebon waters dead. And lo, a stream flows by murmuring like forgetful Acheron. And when I came, the gloom was thick upon the valley, and all was still. But a faint wind had begun to lull the flowers with an eldritch whisper, and from the slow waters rose a low, lone chant. And the flowers in a voiceless antiphony swayed rhythmic: the eldritch wind played upon the flowers of death a dirge, and the dirge was like the cry of a damned thing lost or a lost thing damned, damned and lost through all eternity. And the dirge touched within me some forgotten chord, so that I trembled at the tones. And turning in blind despair, I passed from out the valley.

And as I went, I watched the pall that was the sky above, shifting blacknesses that changed from ebony to jet and pitch to sable, deepening and darkening until the firmament writhed in cosmic torment. For long hours, the skies brooded in their malice and their hate, while I wandered on and on before their sullen blackness should drop out of the deep above and smother me. Yet the towering gloom ever mounted, as if the masses gathered from all the heavens and all the ages; and the masses were hateful. But I wandered on throughout the desolate land. And I was accompanied only by the black skies. And when I had gone leagues and leagues, the skies began to move, and I shivered when I saw the great gulfs above flowing in turbulent motion; and the darkness did not fall, but like a running spatial sea hastened toward the horizon and poured nadirward as if into some colossal and stupendous gulf beyond. And the great torrent of sable rushed with a rapid fury from the skies in a vast cataract that curtained the whole horizon. The skies were uncovered, and the door was open. And they began to smoulder until, at last, they were bare and burning.

I went on, under the glare of that furnace. There was no object in the sky, but the entire heavens were one flame, hot and dull. And the fires bent down on the land I crossed. And the land was no longer desolate. But everywhere under the glowing sky were hot things that rose, languorous and weary. And the flowers grew, tall and beautiful, but weary under the flame; and the blooms were purple and crimson and orange, and they exhaled poisonous perfumes that rose to the aching sky; but the heat of the heavens descended, and the perfumes rose, and the hot flowers swayed under the fire. There were no trees. There was no forest vegetation. But the flowers grew along the way, tall, and hot, and tired. And they looked up at me and sought relief for their suffering. But I had no black to place upon the gold and purple and orange petals, and the perfumes of the blooms arose, hot and evil like an exhalation of a poison that was sweet and scorching. The rocks of that land were red, and burning; the moss about their base was purple, and suffering; the flowers everywhere were weary and beautiful. And yet I could not pick them; for when I touched their petals, they were soft and warm, and the touch of them made me sick, for it was like a lovely silken corruption whence arose exhalations that overpowered. And yet I could scarcely remove my hand from the blooms, for they were like the hot flesh of infants; and when I caressed them, they clung to my palm; and when I tried to withdraw, the heads of the flowers swayed and followed in my palm with the sinister exhalations rising stronger until my hand was beyond their reach; and then they swayed back, tall, and drooping, and frantic under the hot sky. And there was flame above, and there was glare below. And the rocks were molten; and the things that grew were purple and orange and crimson; and the odors in the air were evil and corrupt and poisonous; and the pools along the wayside were stagnant; and the flowers around them drank of the water but found no relief; and the pale growths upon the surface of the pools basked in death under the burning sky, save where livid lichens grew and sent up dank, poisonous odors. And death was in the sky, and death was on the land; but the flowers lived, suffering and hotly beautiful, and died not. They pleaded still, but I caressed them no longer; for their voluptuous petals and colors and perfume drugged my senses and brought up memories that I had buried. And so, I went on, and looked no more upon the tall, languorous flowers; but they were everywhere, weary and poisonous, lifting their feverish faces to the burning sky. But the sky had no mercy, and I had pity for them and their soft, spoiled petals no longer.

Then the heavens died. There was neither glow nor fire above, and I could not see the land. But I vaguely kept on, seeking her whom I had lost, and seeking vainly. My steps were aimless, but the land itself was shrouded. And through the darkness I walked, while the heavens lay in their pall, and the air mourned. And there were things in the air mourning too; phantoms, pale and spectral, weeping; shadows that drifted away into the gloom. There were eyes, great, tearless eyes that turned toward the heavens; there were hands, folded in the obscurity; there were faces, faces of pale, fair women weeping in the gloom, lovely phantom faces drifting; and I sought and sought, but none was familiar; and I looked into them all. And they changed, and even as I looked, they were malicious and sinister; the faces were lovely and beautiful, but avaricious; and the eyes were gleaming, and the lips writhing, and the faces gloated. But I could not avoid them nor shut out their sight; and they came closer, with starved faces hungry and seeking. And they were all strange, and I knew them not; and I shrank from the lips that writhed over the gleaming teeth. And the wall of night encircled me with ring on ring of faces intermingled, blending together and separating again. And the innumerable wild faces were consumed with desire, and a savage hunger for flesh to fill the cruel, gaping mouths. And they drew closer in the darkness, and their eyes gleamed spectrally, and their taloned hands were outstretched, and a smile was on the starved lips. And I threw my arm over my head and ran through the night. And a demoniacal outburst of laughter swept from the furies, and they ringed me closer and closer till the burning eyes shone almost into mine, and the hot breath was on my face, and the cruel lips were close and triumphant, and the talons curved towards me. And then, in the midst of all the malevolent faces, I saw one, dim and shadowy, that saw me not, nor sought; nor was it turned towards me. But it was pale and beautiful, and it faded in the darkness. And I ran towards it and followed it, but, faint and far, it passed beyond my vision in the night. And when I looked around, there were no furies. But the night was strangely dead.

THE BLACK FLAME

Terrible she stood, amid the spaceward pouring gulfs of monstrous flame, immingled with immensities of empty black; untouched and unconsumed with upward surging billows of incandescent splendor rising and rising all around; aloof, supreme, and remote with the awful radiance of abyssal flame in flow and refluence across her alien face; transcendent, with the rapture of flaming chaoses of infinity illuming all her dreadful beauty. And struggling, struggling, ever struggling from the ultimate pits of darkness onward, upward, and for ever toward the radiant goal, through gulf on gulf aeon on everlasting aeon, slowly, tortuously, with panting breath and limbs that fought the titans Time and Space, I rose from farther deeps unplumbed. Age after age, from cosmic darkness through rayless night, I fought my endless way, upheld by one desire, borne on by one aspiration, drawn by one glow, and yet that faint, far glow a universe all of fire and ebony surging in gulfs immense. And so, I came, after stupendous toil through epochs and epochs of time returning in recurrent cycles to her of the immortal loveliness and the terrible beauty in the shifting chorus and response of flame and blackness. But the radiance wherein she stood enshrined and untouched withered like a furious blast from furnaces infernal at my approach, and all my huge labor was in vain; and the gulfs in unison resolved together, flame to ebony and ebony to flame, flowing as one inseparable back to the choral cosmic harmony of dust and dreams. Vainly and vaguely I questioned; but, trembling out of immensity, echoing and reechoing across the now forever undisturbed domain, from realm to realm thrown on across the bleak and blank abyss, all strangely silent now and vacant, came the last bitter echo of a voiceless whisper: "Thou fool! The flame is black!"

THE SHRIEKING HOUSE

Ghastly rose that long shriek under the black sky, a terrible sound that flayed my nerves so that I sought—vainly—to cover my ears. But ever the shriek rose louder to the black and silent sky.

"The house is shrieking," I said, turning to the passersby with a despairing gesture.

But they looked at me wildly, and their faces darkened with horror, and they covered up their eyes with their cowls, hastening by.

"The house is shrieking. Can't you hear it?" I said, and my voice was beseeching.

But their faces were fearsome as they hurried by.

And ever the shriek swelled to the dead sky, pouring from the house in one incessant sound that coursed through my brain with a horrible, torturing monotony. And I turned in despair to the street, but there were no passersby, and the street, and the house, and the sky were black, all black, and dead.

Then I knew that the house shrieked and shrieked for me alone, and I went up to that screaming horror and entered. In a moment I was running through the corridors, and with a frightened apprehension, I raced from garret to cellar of the shrieking house.

The house was quite empty.

THE KINGDOM OF DREAMS

I do not know how I first came to create the Kingdom of Dreams. It may have suddenly flashed into existence sometime when I was feeling unusually disgusted with the world, or it may have had a dual growth for years with no definite birth. However or whenever it originated, it had from then on an existence more real to me than the material life which forms the existence of most people. The happiest days I spent as a child were in the mythical Kingdom of Dreams.

My first excursions into it were, as I remember, tentative and exploratory, but they steadily became more and more deliberate, and of longer and longer duration, until my life was almost equally divided between a tiresome routine on a place called Earth and a timeless and spaceless wandering through the Kingdom of Dreams. I think my first introductions came externally from the many books I read, but as I became more and more familiar with the empire, I must have assumed the sway myself and moulded it to my own desires, for it was not long until I could enter it at will no matter where I was or what I was doing.

There was no limit to the emerald sea about the isle. It stretched on and on until it vanished, infinitely distant, in the azure horizon. A curtain of haze sometimes hung low upon the horizon, but there was nothing behind it save the ceaseless expanse of waters. My entrance to the Kingdom of Dreams was always by that sea. I found myself steering a boat with one great, white sail, a boat that scudded across the waves with a wild and eager swiftness. A fresh wind blew cool at my back and drove the boat always at that wild speed. The sea was sprinkled with foam; the waves washed rhythmically and filled the air with their eternal murmur, or they lapped softly on the boat when it dipped and skimmed onward, but the sea never became stormy. The scene itself was usually the same: the dome of the sky azure and clear except for a few high, fleecy clouds, the sea freshening under the breeze, and the boat scudding across the waves.

I invariably guided the boat to one spot, a small cove whose waters were crystal-clear and in whose depths grew frail corals amid strange sea-growths. I landed on a spot where the beach was soft and white, let the boat drift as it wished, and set out.

The Kingdom of Dreams was an enchanted isle set in foam-flecked seas of emerald, but an isle which I never completely explored because nothing ever showed itself twice to me. I could not find again the things I once had seen. Nothing existed in the Kingdom except that which was beautiful; but nothing whose pleasure has once been tasted can longer be beautiful, and so the realm was forever unexplored though I travelled there long hours. All that I saw became lost immediately, a fading memory before the new and unexperienced pleasures I found to take their place.

I remember one of the first—perhaps the first—of my wanderings. I found myself walking along a road paved with a smooth, black stone. Ahead, under the glare of a burning sun that was yet not uncomfortable, rose the spires and domes of a city that shone like molten brass. The air was still and hot; no sound save the musical hum of some insect broke the silence. I went up to a massive door that guarded the entrance to the city. No keeper was there, but none was needed, for at my approach the door separated in the middle and the halves slid into the walls with a brazen clang. When I had passed through, they flew together again with another metallic ring.

Quaint and curious houses, all joined together, lined the street down which I was passing. I entered none though they looked deserted. But the houses gradually became bigger and queerer until I was walking between oriental edifices crowned with spires and minarets. The rows ended, the street abruptly turned—and I found myself before a mighty palace all built of crystal and marble. I went up to the castle; the doors opened silently even as I approached, and I passed in without halting. The doors closed behind me. Instantly, two black leopards padded up to me from either side of the doors and took up their station with me. I walked down the marble floor of the hall with the sleek leopards, who crept a little ahead and to one side of me.

And then I began to explore the palace, led by the watchful leopards. For hours I wandered through its never-ending succession of halls, each filled with strange treasures; for hours I passed into room after room, regretting even as I passed that I could not linger; for hours I reveled in the hoards of the castle until I seemed to be watching a continually shifting pageant of the gods. There was a long hall filled with countless many-colored silken tapestries that rustled softly as I passed. There was a chamber fantastically wrought from one enormous emerald that blazed with its own secret fire; and in that chamber was naught save a teakwood chest filled with perfect stones from the heart of the jewel. Remote from all the rest I found a little, dark room that had upon a table of ebony a priceless flask of wine made by unknown hands long ago and left aging in this room ever since. I tasted it, and its very taste was pain for I knew that when I left, the room would be lost to me forever. And so I replaced the the flask of blood-red wine that I might always recall with greater joy the pleasure I had not experienced. I found a hall of splashing colours wonderful, of gold and green and purple, of ruby, jet, and blue, that melted and blended in a restless prismatic splendour. And in an isolated crypt I came upon a nameless, fearful instrument playing the nameless, fearful anthem of Antares, a melody from which I fled, frantically trying to stop my ears, until I had fled the castle, fled the isle, and fled the sea.

UNFORGOTTEN NIGHT

I remember how I tossed and rolled, unable to sleep, on that night long ago. I remember how the slow hours passed, bringing only a growing restlessness. I remember how my nervousness grew upon me, stronger and stronger, for I knew that I *must* go out. And I recall how late—late in that night I arose, dressed, and went out. Yet I do not know what I saw when I first left the lonely farmhouse; I do not know what I saw in the later hours of that strange walk. I remember but one scene, clear and ghastly, which has obliterated all else.

I had come to a pause on a short bridge that crossed a dark, stagnant pool. Behind me lay a narrow road, thick with the moon's pallor. On either side stretched a forest, still and fearful, a forest that was not solid but somewhat open near the road so that I looked into its depths and fancied I saw things move. But across the bridge, the entire country spread before me until its low hills faded into the night. There were no trees on the other side of the pond, but only grass or occasional bushes among the rocks and boulders strewn through it. I glanced up once—and once only. A huge wan moon was creeping across the sky, casting a deathliness on all it touched. A few haggard wisps of cloud hung motionless and leprous in the air. To the south the heavens were dimly and darkly luminous, but to the north they were completely empty with a sinister, a malignant blackness. The stars were shining coldly, but their whiteness intensified the ebon horror of the skies.

Nothing lived in all that utter solitude. There came no sound from the forest; no murmur rose from the dead waters beneath; a maddening and appalling silence crouched upon the land. And the stealthy silence seemed only to deepen when the low and rhythmic cadence of my steps again fell upon the road.

SANTON MERLIN

Santon Merlin was the epitome of a master of the black arts. In Amenti, he could have superseded Thoth, for he had the wisdom of thirty centuries added to the knowledge and accumulated lore that made Thoth the god of magic. Had he ever turned loose the ancient and long-forgotten forces over which he had gained control, had he ever evoked them from astrology, necromancy, and the kabalistic rituals by his own secret incantations, there would have come again to earth, but in reality, what Breughel the Elder engraved centuries ago. All the saintly would have been blotted out, and all that was pure defiled in a perpetual sabbat.

He was tall and slim, of an extreme and almost deathly pallor; but his unnatural paleness was subordinate and accentuating to his eyes.

The man himself, and all his soul and mind were enclosed in those eyes. They were larger than is usual, but deep-set and surrounded by dark rings, the rings not of dissipation, but of profound research in a field which has been neglected for hundreds of years. They were strange and haunting eyes, and they had properties of a kind I have never found elsewhere. I have watched them for half an hour, and only seen a white face with two dark circles; and I have then seen them begin to glow and melt until they gleamed blackly liquid, hinting of mysterious rites and forbidden knowledge. It was as if he had been thinking of sorcery, became aware that he was watched, opened up his eyes in a blaze of hate to lay some hypnotic spell upon the intruder, and then, contemptuous of wasting his time on a minor subject, had withdrawn again into his mind. Yet it did not seem that he dropped his lids, but that his eyes possessed some extraordinary power by which they could at times let through the light of the mind, and at others shut up Santon Merlin within himself.

His hair was thick and so dark as to appear almost black; it was neither combed nor unkempt, but shoved back as if from running his hands through it while absorbed in some rare Latin work on demonology.

Neither his lips nor any other part of his face stood out. To be sure, you knew in a vague way that his forehead was high and pale, that his lips were thin and had a sardonic droop, but these were noticed only inasmuch as they intensified the overwhelming supremacy of his eyes.

His very presence suggested the nature of his studies. When he entered a room, something heavy and blighting seemed to creep in with him, an effluence of utter and transcendent evil. Before a beholder knew anything about Santon Merlin, there arose in his mind thoughts of witchcraft, the occult sciences, and outlawed rites in secret places. In a violated crypt, with a brazier before him lighting up hieroglyphs and symbols marked on the floor, with a yellowed manuscript between his hands, and with his eyes burning feverishly while he murmured an incantation, he could have taken the place of the Prince of Darkness.

On his left hand, setting off his long and tapering white fingers, he wore the one stone that was adequate, a ring set with a great emerald. Like Santon Merlin, it was dull and lustreless under an unfavourable light; but in the proper environment the jewel blazed into flame as mysterious and sinister as he who possessed it.

A Legend of Yesterday

We, the kings Eternity, Infinity and Death, rulers of the Cosmic Dust unbounded, changeless, motionless, and sempiternal, met in solemn conclave now in this central hall of our abysmal, black, and measureless domain, far-travelling across the shrouded void from the outer portions of our dominion, are come, within the midmost portion of our sway, to settle once and for all the rumour floating through the Cosmic Dust submissive; for, arising we know not whence nor how, hath come this whisper, dark and almost meaningless; and this whisper is that long ago there was no Cosmic Dust, but instead great solid spheres of matter; and some of these had light, and others life; but all this is beyond the memory of us, the trinity eternal and omnipotent, sovereigns of all hitherto, henceforth, and forever, and in no crypt of our memory nor page of our history can we discover any such change in the Cosmic Dust, and hardly are these terms intelligible to us; but furthermore, the rumour saith that what was once, again shall be, and that the Cosmic Dust will stir and shape itself while gathering forces build anew what it saith the Cosmic Dust once was: a Universe; inconceivable and unimaginable are the thoughts of this, even the thought that this ever could have been; for the Cosmic Dust is motionless, and was motionless, and motionless shall be, black, submissive, void of life and light and sound; always, in so far as we remember, hath it been thus, and we who are timeless and deathless would recall the mutations of our realm, but we hold no memory of such; and now we are just come from travelling in our farther empire, but we have found no answer there; and from dominion to dominion and immensity to immensity, measureless and appalling, wherein the least space is unguessable, untellable, and staggering even to our infinite intelligence, we have travelled through the lifeless lightless soundless universal pall of Cosmic Dust, but we have found no answer; and we therefore judge: now have we proved that the Cosmic Dust is everywhere and was everywhere throughout all our memory and all our realm; and the terms life and light are meaningless, and no such thing as a universe has ever existed; and what has not been can not be again; for life, and light, and time, and matter are whispers, only whispers.

FROM "THE TOWER OF SOUND"

At first I could not tell what it was that had broken my sleep, but an apprehension and nervousness filled me so that I became wide awake almost instantly. And it was not long until I realized that all the sounds to which I had grown accustomed in my stay at the tower were changed, and that among them were new tones oddly menacing. The entire castle was filled with an innumerable patter, an utterly dreadful scampering as if a horde of rats swept through the walls and passages. And those sounds as of the rush of countless tiny feet were increasing even as I listened, until they became inseparable in an ever-rising whisper that fled through the house. Far away I heard the wind howl and rage about the castle, and from the bottom of the cliff thundered upward the incessant roar of the sea. But the sounds came to me muffled through the walls of the castle, and served only to intensify the whispers in the halls. And that whisper, that indescribable sound that reigned within the castle, was all the more appalling for I knew the castle was kept shut at night to keep out the wind which then blew strong on the cliff. It was as if the passages themselves were whispering.

I jumped out of bed and ran to the door of my room. I opened it cautiously and peered out. The hall was alive with gusts of wind, gusts that came from no particular direction but eddied from side to side, or formed little whirlpools, or swept aimlessly about. The air seemed to be stirring of itself, and had, in the way it was beginning to sweep down the hall, a wild, a frenzied note that infused in me a kind of panic.

AN EPITAPH ON JUPITER

"Here lingers the memory of him whose birthplace we know not, whose coming was as great a riddle as his passing. His age, his nature, his life, we cannot tell. This monolith is erected to the unknown who will forever remain a baffling mystery.

"We found him wandering by the dead waters of a tarn. In no part of his being did we recognize that with which we were familiar. His lips were sealed, for he spoke not our tongue, nor we, his. Whence he came is unknown. Why he came is a secret. His manner of coming can never be disclosed for he who alone knew shall speak no more.

"His world was alien, a remote planet in the outer gulfs. He trembled when we came upon him, for even as he to us were we strange to him. The lethal waters frightened him. The purple vegetation appalled him. He shrank from the cryptic riddles of our world and found only desolation in things he could not comprehend. We were kind to him, but the barrier between us was impenetrable. We gave him sustenance, but he wasted away for lack of what we could not supply.

"His eyes were stricken with the light of what he saw and the memory of what he left. He sought peace in the skies but found no single star he knew. His inward griefs consumed him. He died, madly peering into unfamiliar heavens for the world whence he came.

"His ashes were strewn on the nightward and spaceward flowing winds. Perhaps his dust, drifting we know not whither toward what secret abysms of the universe, will come to that singular region whence he started on his mighty pilgrimage.

"Let no hand contaminate his tomb. He was apart from us, and we from him. His grief is ended, but the riddle lingers on. Forget not, ye who wander here."

COMMENTARY

Abbreviations

BM   *Broken Mirrors*
C   *Colossus*
CP   *Collected Poems*
DD   *Don't Dream*
DM   *Dark of the Moon,* ed. August Derleth (Sauk City, WI: Arkham House, 1947)
DO   *Dark Odyssey*
DWM   *A Donald Wandrei Miscellany*
E   *Ecstasy and Other Poems*
EF   *The Eye and the Finger*
FSC   *Fire and Sleet and Candlelight,* ed. August Derleth (Sauk City, WI: Arkham House, 1961)
JHL   John Hay Library, Brown University
MTS   *Mysteries of Time and Spirit*
PM   *Poems for Midnight*
WT   *Weird Tales*

Books

Broken Mirrors (with Francis Bosworth, Karl Litzenberg, Gordon Louis Roth, and Harrison Salisbury; illustrated by Leo Henkora). [St. Paul, MN:] Avon Press, 1928. [Texts derived from a typescript at JHL.]

Collected Poems. Edited by S. T. Joshi. West Warwick, RI: Necronomicon Press, 1988.

Colossus: The Collected Science Fiction of Donald Wandrei. Edited by Philip J. Rahman and Dennis E. Weiler. Minneapolis, MN: Fedogan & Bremer, 1989.

Dark Odyssey. With Five Illustrations by Howard Wandrei. St. Paul, MN: Webb Publishing Co., [1931].

A Donald Wandrei Miscellany. Edited by D. H. Olson. St. Paul. MN: Sidecar Preservation Society, 2001.

Don't Dream: The Collected Horror and Fantasy of Donald Wandrei. Edited by Philip J. Rahman and Dennis E. Weiler. Minneapolis, MN: Fedogan & Bremer, 1997.

Ecstasy and Other Poems. Athol, MA: Recluse Press, 1928.

The Eye and the Finger. Sauk City, WI: Arkham House, 1944.

Mysteries of Time and Spirit: The Letters of H. P. Lovecraft and Donald Wandrei. Edited by S. T. Joshi and David E. Schultz. San Francisco: Night Shade Books, 2002.

Poems for Midnight. Sauk City, WI: Arkham House, 1964.

Poems

After Bacchus, Eros. In *DO.*

Aftermath. In *BM.*

Amphitrite. In *E.* In Greek myth, Amphitrite (pronounced am-fi-trī′-tā) was a sea-maiden known as a Nereid, and the wife of Poseidon.

Aphrodite. In *E.*

At the Bacchic Revel. In *E.* See "Bacchanalia."

Aubade. In *DO.* In music, "aubade" (from the French *aube,* dawn) is a composition to be played in the early morning.

Awakening. In *E.*

Bacchanalia. In *E.* The Bacchanalia was a Greek-derived festival practiced in Rome in the third and second centuries B.C.E.; devoted to Bacchus (the Roman counterpart of Dionysus), the festivals became notorious for their debauchery and were banned by a decree of the Senate in 186 B.C.E. For another poem on roughly the same subject, see "At the Bacchic Revel."

Black Flame. First published in *DD.*

Borealis. In *DO, PM.*

The Challenger. *Minnesota Quarterly* 4, No. 3 (Spring 1927): 36. In *E, PM.* Perhaps the first of Wandrei's poems expressing cosmicism.

Chant to the Dead. *Minnesota Quarterly* 4, No. 3 (Spring 1927): 34.

Chaos Resolved. In *DO.*

The Classicist. In *DWM.* Published during Wandrei's years at the University of Minnesota (1926–31). "P. V." is unidentified.

The Corpse Speaks. *Midwest Student* (May 1927) (as "In the Grave"). *The Recluse* No. 1 (1927): 76 (as "In the Grave"). In *PM.* One of Wandrei's signature pieces. For a very different poem using a similar metre, see "I Am Man" (p. 139).

Corroding Acids. *Minnesota Quarterly* 7, No. 2 (Winter 1929): 31.

Credo. In *BM.*

The Cypress-Bog. *WT* 16, No. 5 (November 1930): 714.

Dark Odyssey. In *DO, PM*.

Dead Fruit of the Fugitive Years. *Minnesota Quarterly* 7, No. 2 (Winter 1929): 27–31.

The Dead Mistress. In *BM*. The typescript used as the copy-text presents substantial revisions from the printed text.

The Deadly Calm. *Minnesota Quarterly* 7, No. 2 (Winter 1929): 30.

Death and the Poet: A Fragment. In *E*. Substantially revised as "Death and the Traveler: A Fragment" (p. 83). In l. 4, "Acherontic" refers to Acheron, one of the five rivers in the Greek underworld. In l. 5, "Hadean" is an adjectival form of Hades, the god of the underworld (also known as Pluto). "Hades" is not the name of the Greek underworld, although many Greek writers refer to "in Hades" as a shorthand for "in [the house of] Hades." In l. 21, "Lethean" is the adjectival form of Lethe, another river in the underworld. In l. 30, "Paphian" is the adjectival form of Paphos, a city on Cyprus where Aphrodite was reputed to have been born. See the prose poem "Paphos" (p. 105).

Death and the Traveler: A Fragment. In *PM*. A revised version of "Death and the Poet: A Fragment" (p. 34).

The Death of the Flowers. First published in *DWM*. For the date of the work, see note on "Ebony and Silver."

The Dream. *Minnesota Quarterly* 7, No. 1 (Fall 1929): 30.

The Dream Changes. *Minnesota Quarterly* 7, No. 2 (Winter 1929): 27. In l. 4, "Nielsen" refers to the Danish artist Kai Nielsen (1882–1924). The last two lines deliberately echo Poe's celebrated poem "Dream-Land" (1844), ll. 6–7: "From a wild weird clime that lieth, sublime, / Out of Space—out of Time."

The Dream That Dies. In *PM*. An extensive revision of "The Voice of Beauty" (p. 23).

Dreaming Away My Life. First published in *DD*. Probably written in 1927–28. On p. 159, "Acheron" is one of the five rivers in the Greek underworld.

Drink! In *BM*.

A Drinking Song. In *E*. A drinking song that evokes Bacchus, the Roman god of wine (see "Bacchanalia").

Ebony and Silver. First published in *DWM*. In a letter to Lovecraft dated 6 April 1927, Wandrei writes: "I have written two more poems in prose, at least one of which is fairly good, and which I shall send you soon. It is called 'The Death of the Flowers'. I don't like the other, which will be called 'Black and Silver' or 'Ebony and Silver', and am surprised at myself for writing it"

(*MTS* 70). Wandrei's surprise may derive from the unusually explicit sexual imagery in the work.

Ecstasy. In *E*.

Elegy. First published in *DWM*. Wandrei has appended a note: "For Msgr. Joseph A. Ertel, March 12, 1974."

Epilude. In *DO*. The term "epilude" is evidently a coinage by Wandrei, perhaps similar in meaning to "postlude" (a closing piece of music).

An Epitaph on Jupiter. Date of composition unknown; probably 1927 or 1928. Published in the *Arkham Collector* No. 7 (Summer 1970): 219–20.

Epitaph to a Lady. *Minnesota Quarterly* 9, No. 3 (Spring 1932): 54–55.

Epithalamium. In *DO*. An epithalamium (Greek for "before the bridal chamber") is a nuptial song.

Fata Morgana. In *DO*. The title is the Italian form of the name Morgan le Fay, the shape-shifting half-sister of the wizard Merlin. The term is also used to refer to mirages seen at sea, the result of a temperature inversion.

The Five Lords. In *DO*.

Fling Wide the Roses. In *BM*.

For the Perishing Aphrodite. In *DO*. In l. 10, "chloral" is short for chloral hydrate, a soporific.

Forest Shapes. In *FSC*, *PM*.

From the Shadowlands of Memory. In *E*. The title may be meant to echo Clark Ashton Smith's prose poem "From the Crypts of Memory" (1917; in *Ebony and Crystal* [1922]).

From "The Tower of Sound." First published in *DWM*. Perhaps no more than an account of a dream.

Futility. In *E*. For "Paphian" (l. 14), see note on "Death and the Poet: A Fragment."

The Glow. *Minnesota Quarterly* 7, No. 1 (Fall 1929): 27–28.

Golden Poppy. Circulated by Wandrei to colleagues on 25 August 1978. On the top of the page Wandrei has given the date of composition: "Aug. 19, 1978 / First draft."

The Greatest Regret. In *E*. Perhaps a reflection of Wandrei's admiration of Clark Ashton Smith's ability to draw and paint his fantastic conceptions.

Hermaphroditus. In *E*. In Greek myth, Hermaphroditus was the son of Hermes and Aphrodite who in some artwork was depicted as having female breasts and a male phallus. Wandrei's poem may allude to *The Hermaphrodite* (1926) by Samuel Loveman (1887–1976), a long poem evoking classical Greece.

I Am Man. Circulated by Wandrei to colleagues on 25 August 1978. At the top of the page Wandrei has given the date of composition: "First draft November 4, 1977 / Revised June 25, 1978." He has deliberately used the same metrical scheme as "The Corpse Speaks," but for a very different purpose.

In Mandrikor. In *E, PM*. (The version in *E* is found under "Uncollected Poems.")

In Memoriam: George Sterling. In *E, PM*. Sterling (1869–1926), a leading California poet of the period, was the poetic mentor of Clark Ashton Smith and assisted Smith significantly in the publication of his first four volumes of poetry, *The Star-Treader and Other Poems* (1912), *Odes and Sonnets* (1918), *Ebony and Crystal* (1922), and *Sandalwood* (1925). He died by his own hand on 17 November 1926. Wandrei does not appear to have been personally acquainted with Sterling, as no correspondence between the two writers survives.

In Memoriam: No Name. In *DO, PM*.

Incubus. In *PM*.

Ishmael. *College Verse* (March 1932). In *PM*. Ishmael is mentioned in Genesis (16f.) as the son of Abraham and the maidservant Hagar. Ishmael and his mother were later banished and wandered the wilderness of Beersheeba. Ishmael later became the father of twelve tribal chieftains.

King of the Shadowland. In *PM*.

The Kingdom of Dreams. First published in *DD*. An autobiographical work, perhaps recording actual dreams that Wandrei had. A sequel to this work, "Lotus and Poppy" (*DD* 354–56), is manifestly an autobiographical essay recording Wandrei's discovery of Clark Ashton Smith and other weird writers.

Largo. In *DO*. In music, "largo" (Italian for "slow") is a tempo indication.

A Legend of Yesterday. *Leaves* No. 1 (Summer 1937): 79. Published along with "The Twilight of Time" (the original title of "The Red Brain," *WT*, October 1927) and "On the Threshold of Eternity," and comprising a kind of "Cosmic Dust" trilogy. The first two were included in *EF* and *C*, but "A Legend of Yesterday" is previously unreprinted.

Let Us Love To-night. In *E*. See "To Myrrhiline" (p. 31) for another poem possibly addressed to the same woman, if indeed Wandrei had a specific woman in mind.

[Limerick]. Included in a letter to August Derleth, 19 April 1937 (ms., State Historical Society of Wisconsin, Madison, WI).

Lines. Circulated by Wandrei to colleagues on 17 September 1978. See "Solitary."

The Little Gods Wait. *WT* 20, No. 1 (July 1932): 116.

Look Homeward, Angel. In *DO*, *PM*. The title is taken from a line in Milton's "Lycidas" (1637), l. 163: "Look homeward, Angel, and melt with ruth."

Lost Atlantis. *Minnesota Quarterly* 4, No. 3 (Spring 1927): 34–35. In *DO*, *PM*.

The Lost Moon. Read by Lovecraft (as cited in a letter to Wandrei, 15 February 1928; *MTS* 204), hence presumably enclosed in a letter to Lovecraft of 31 January 1928. Published in the *Arkham Collector* No. 7 (Summer 1970): 218–19. In *DWM*.

Lyrics of Doubt. *Minnesota Quarterly* 7, No. 3 (Spring 1930): 83–85.

Marmora. *WT* 15, No. 5 (May 1930): 636. Wandrei intends "Marmora" as an imaginary realm, but *marmor* is Latin for "marble" (cf. l. 6).

The Messengers. *Minnesota Quarterly* 4, No. 1 (Fall 1926): 58–59. In *EF*, *DD*. In a letter to Lovecraft, Wandrei mentions the inspiration of this prose poem and "The Pursuers": "It was a sultry day, hot and dusty; great dust storms were sweeping over the prairies, and finally reached the Twin Cities. All that day, the air was so dusty that you could not see beyond a block; the sky smouldered, and the sun was suggested only by a dull and dark glow; everything was phantasmal in the pall, and the effect of that brooding, smoking sky with the sun a red and inflamed eye was depressing beyond measure. It was as if the heavens were burning, as if some great conflagration were raging beyond the obscuring dust-pall out in space" (*MTS* 72).

The Monster Gods. Found in chapter 9 of *Dead Titans, Waken!* (ms., John Hay Library, Brown University), the original version of *The Web of Easter Island* (Sauk City, WI: Arkham House, 1948). The novel was written between Oct. 1930 and Dec. 1931. In *The Web of Easter Island*, a slightly revised version of the fourth stanza appears (p. 116). In both versions, the poem is said to have been written by the British poet Aubrey Lellith (in *Dead Titans* it is said to have appeared in the poetry journal *Helicon*), and is meant to indicate the psychological effect upon sensitive temperaments of the imminent return of the Titans (as in H. P. Lovecraft's "The Call of Cthulhu").

Moon Magic. *Minnesota Quarterly* 7, No. 1 (Fall 1929): 27–30.

The Moon-Glen Altar. In *BM*, *PM*.

The Morning of a Nymph. *College Verse* (March 1932). In *PM*.

Morning Song. In *DO*.

My Lady Hath Two Lovely Lips. In *BM*.

The Night Wind. In *DO*.

Nightmare. In *E*. An early version of "Nightmare in Green," which was inserted into the sequence *Sonnets of the Midnight Hours*.

On Some Drawings. In *E*, *PM*. In l. 10, Lilith was reputed to be Adam's first wife; she later came to be the embodiment of witchcraft and evil.

The One Who Died. First published in *DWM*. This is possibly the prose poem that Wandrei refers to in several letters to Lovecraft under the title "Beyond the Milky Way." In a letter of 17 April 1927, he notes the genesis of the story "The Shadow of a Nightmare" (*WT*, May 1929): "The third idea was of something existing, either visibly or in memory, from incredibly ancient times. The end of the story is bodily removed from another that I wrote about two years ago, entitled 'Beyond the Milky Way'. It was a mess" (*MTS* 84). If Wandrei is correct on the date of the story, it must have been written in 1925.

The Overtone. *Minnesota Quarterly* 7, No. 1 (Fall 1929): 29.

Paphos. First published in *CP*. Enclosed in a letter to Clark Ashton Smith, 25 March 1927 (ms., Clark Ashton Smith Papers, John Hay Library, Brown University). Wandrei has rendered the title in Greek capitals (ΠΑΦΟΣ). For the name, see note on "Death and the Poet: A Fragment."

Pedagogues. In *DWM*. Published during Wandrei's years at the University of Minnesota (1926–31). In l. 3, "Major Hooples" refers to Major Amos B. Hoople, a character in the popular comic strip "Our Boarding House," by Gene Ahern, which began publication in 1921. In l. 11, "Alfred" refers to Alfred the Great (849?–899), king of Wessex (871–99). In l. 22, "ge" is a particle in Greek; "isdem" is a form of the Latin word *idem* ("the same"). In l. 29, "Firkins" may refer to Oscar W. Firkins (1864–1932), a prolific academic literary critic.

Phantom. *Minnesota Quarterly* 7, No. 3 (Spring 1930): 83 (as "Op. 561"; as part of "Lyrics of Doubt"). In *PM*.

Philomela. In *E*. In Greek myth, Philomela and Procne were the daughters of Pandion, a king of Athens. Procne was married to Tereus, king of Thrace, but Tereus fell in love with Philomela and, after raping her, cut out her tongue and hid her in a fortress. She was later turned into a swallow and Procne into a nightingale. Latin authors state that Philomela was turned into a nightingale and Procne into a swallow; Wandrei follows this legendry.

The Plague Ship. In *DO*, *PM*.

[Poems from *Invisible Sun*]. *Invisible Sun* (ms., John Hay Library, Brown University) is an autobiographical mainstream novel written between Sept. 1932 and Jan. 1933. The first poem ("I am as mad as can be . . .") appears in chapter 32 and is said to have been composed by one of the protagonists of the novel, Sven, after an encounter with a character named only The Fool. The second poem ("Dig and delve . . .") is spoken by The Fool in chapter 49. The limerick appears in chapter 62 and is spoken by a college student named Bob during a sex party.

The Poet's Lament. In *DWM*. Published during Wandrei's years at the University of Minnesota (1926–31).

The Poet's Language. In *E*.

Portrait of a Lady During a Half Hour Wait While She Finished Dressing. *Minnesota Quarterly* 9, No. 3 (Spring 1932): 55. In l. 1, "Wedgwood" refers to high-quality pottery manufactured by British craftsman Josiah Wedgwood (1730–1795) and his successors. In the original text the name is spelled "Wedgewood." Also in l. 1, "saki" (more appropriately "sake") is the Japanese alcoholic drink made from rice. In ll. 5–6, Wandrei refers to the edition of Lewis Carroll's *Alice's Adventures in Wonderland* (1929) illustrated by Willy Pogány (1882–1955). In l. 6, "Rothenstein" refers to British portrait painter William Rothenstein (1889–1925). In l. 7, Wandrei refers to the edition of Poe's *Tales of Mystery and Imagination* (1919) illustrated by Harry Clarke (1889–1931). In l. 8 Wandrei refers to celebrated Welsh fantaisiste Arthur Machen (1863–1947). In l. 9 Wandrei refers to cosmeticist Elizabeth Arden (1878–1966); Madame Ganna Walska (born Hanna Puacz, 1887–1984), a Polish opera singer who created a large estate and botanical garden near Santa Barbara, California, called Lotusland; and Helena Rubinstein (not Rubenstein) (1872–1965), Polish-American cosmeticist.

The Prehistoric Huntsman. In *FSC, PM*.

The Purple Land. First published in *DD*. The work was read by Lovecraft on 15 February 1928 (MTS 204), hence was presumably sent to Lovecraft in Wandrei's letter of 31 January 1928.

The Pursuers. *Minnesota Quarterly* 4, No. 1 (Fall 1926): 59. In *EF, DD*. For the inspiration of this prose poem, see note on "The Messengers."

A Queen in Other Skies. *WT* 19, No. 1 (January 1932): 109. The metrical scheme here is similar to that used in "Phantom" (p. 79).

Red. In *E, PM*.

Sanctity and Sin. In *E*.

Santon Merlin. First published in *DD*. In l. 1, "Amenti" refers to the abode of the dead in Egyptian mythology, where souls are judged by Osiris. On p. 156, "Breughel the Elder" refers to Pieter Breughel the Elder (1525?–1569), celebrated Dutch painter and engraver. In the original text, the name is misspelled "Breghuel."

Satiation. In *E*.

The School of Seduction. Included in a letter to August Derleth, 16 November 1927 (ms., State Historical Society of Wisconsin, Madison, WI). Wandrei has added a note: "Please do not take this gem as representative of my lyrical escapes."

The Second Beauty. *Minnesota Quarterly* 7, No. 2 (Winter 1929): 28.

September Hill. First published in *DWM*. The poem was written on the sixty-eighth anniversary of the birth of Wandrei's brother Howard (1909–1956), 24 September 1977. The setting is the family gravesite in Acacia Cemetery, St. Paul.

Shadowy Night. In *PM*.

The Shrieking House. First published in *DD*.

The Sleeper. In *BM, PM*.

Solitary. Circulated (along with "Lines") by Wandrei to colleagues on 17 September 1978. At the top of the page Wandrei has dated the poem as follows: "First drafts September, 1977 / Revised September 15, 1978."

Somewhere Past Ispahan. In *PM*. Ispahan is a city in Persia (now Isfahan or Esfahan in Iran) was founded by the Elamites and was later occupied by the Sassanids, Arsacids, and Parthians. It became a leading city under the Arabs; in the 16th century it became the capital of the Safavid dynasty. In 1722 it was raided by the Afghans and largely destroyed. In l. 34 the name "Cyrenaya" is presumably meant to evoke Cyrene, a Greek city in Libya. In l. 88, "champak" refers to champac or champak, an East Indian tree yielding fragrant yellow flowers.

The Song. *Minnesota Quarterly* 7, No. 1 (Fall 1929): 28–29.

Song of Autumn. *Minnesota Quarterly* 4, No. 1 (Fall 1926): 15 (as "The Song of Autumn"). In *E* (as "The Song of Autumn"), *PM*. Awarded honorable mention in the Witter Bynner Undergraduate Poetry Prize for 1926.

Song of Oblivion. *Minnesota Quarterly* 4, No. 3 (Spring 1927): 33 (as "The Song of Oblivion"). In *E* (as "The Song of Oblivion"), *PM*.

Sonnets of the Midnight Hours.
    After Sleep. In *DM, PM*.
    As I Remember. *WT* 12, No. 3 (September 1928): 374.
    The Bell. In *DM, PM*.
    Capture. In *DM, PM*.
    The Cocoon. In *DM, PM*.
    The Creatures. *WT* 12, No. 5 (November 1928): 624. Early version of "The Prey."

Doom. *WT* 13, No. 2 (February 1929): 254.

Dream-Horror. *WT* 11, No. 5 (May 1928): 674. Early version of "In the Pit."

Escape. In *DM, PM.*

The Eye. *WT* 12, No. 1 (July 1928): 69. In *DM, PM.*

Fantastic Sculpture. In *PM.*

The Grip of Evil Dreams. *WT* 12, No. 2 (August 1928): 231. Early version of "The Creatures."

The Head. *WT* 12, No. 6 (December 1928): 815. In *DM, PM.*

The Hungry Flowers. *WT* 11, No. 5 (May 1928): 674. In *DM, PM.*

In the Attic. In *DM, PM.*

In the Pit. In *DM, PM.* A revision of "Dream-Horror."

The Little Creature. In *DM, PM.* A revision of "The Grip of Evil Dreams."

The Metal God. In *DM, PM.*

Monstrous Form. In *PM.*

Nightmare in Green. In *PM.* A revision of "Nightmare" (p. 46).

The Old Companions. In *DM, PM.*

The Pool. In *DM, PM.*

The Prey. In *DM, PM.* A revision of "The Creatures."

Purple. *WT* 11, No. 6 (June 1928): 837. In *DM, PM.*

The Rack. In *DM, PM.*

The Red Specter. *WT* 13, No. 1 (January 1929): 110.

The Statues. *WT* 12, No. 4 (October 1928): 480. In *DM, PM.*

The Torturers. In *DM, PM.*

The Tree. In *PM.*

The Ultimate Vision. In *DM, PM.* A revision of "A Vision of the Future."

The Unknown Color. In *PM.*

A Vision of the Future. *WT* 13, No. 3 (March 1929): 420. Early version of "The Ultimate Vision."

What Followed Me? In *PM.*

Street Scene. In *DWM.* Published during Wandrei's years at the University of Minnesota (1926–31).

Surrender. *Minnesota Quarterly* 7, No. 2 (Winter 1929): 27.

A Testament of Desertion. *Minnesota Quarterly* 7, No. 3 (Spring 1930): 83–84.

There Was a Smell of Dandelions. In *DWM.* Published during Wandrei's years at the University of Minnesota (1926–31). A parody of poetry published in the *Minnesota Quarterly*, the college's student literary magazine. Hjalmar Bjornson was one of Wandrei's best friends in college.

This Larger Room. *Minnesota Quarterly* 7, No. 2 (Winter 1929): 29.

Though All My Days. *Minnesota Quarterly* 7, No. 2 (Winter 1929): 28.

To Lucasta on Her Birthday. In *DO*. The title alludes to the Lucasta poems (specifically "To Lucasta: Going to the Wars") by the British poet Richard Lovelace (1618–1657/58)

To Myrrhiline. In *E*.

To the God of My Fathers. *Minnesota Quarterly* 7, No. 3 (Spring 1930): 85.

Twice Excellent Perfection. *Minnesota Quarterly* 7, No. 2 (Winter 1929): 29.

Under the Grass. In *DO*, *PM*.

Unforgotten Night. First published in *DD*. Perhaps an account of a dream by Wandrei.

Vain Warning. In *E*.

Valerian. In *E*. A tribute to Wandrei's poetic mentor, Clark Ashton Smith (1893–1961). As a noun, *valerian* is an herb that can be used as a purgative or sedative. The poem utilizes the exotic vocabulary for which Smith became famous (and notorious). Such terms as "Hylots of Calair" (l. 14), "Mirtylon" (l. 18), "Serise" (l. 32), and "Atthla" (l. 37) are imaginary.

Villanelle à la Mode. In *DO*. A villanelle is a verse form that usually has five tercets (three-line stanzas) and a quatrain, the second lines of each stanza utilizing the same rhyme. Wandrei has followed this scheme. In l. 13, "aquarelle" is a drawing in watercolour. In l. 14, "brede" is an archaic term for an embroidery, "breve" is a type of note in music.

The Voice of Beauty. In *E*. Later revised as "The Dream That Dies" (p. 80).

The Voyagers' Return to Tyre. In *DO* (as "Heraclydion's Return from the Golden Journey"), *PM*. Tyre was a city in what is now Lebanon founded by the Phoenicians c. 1300 B.C.E. Its location on the eastern coast of the Mediterranean made it an important seaport in antiquity. It was conquered by Alexander the Great in 332 B.C.E.

Water Sprite. In *FSC*, *PM*.

The Whispering Knoll. In *DO*, *PM*.

Witches' Sabbath. In *PM*.

With Cat-like Tread. *Minnesota Quarterly* 7, No. 2 (Winter 1929): 31.

The Woman Answers. *Minnesota Quarterly* 7, No. 2 (Winter 1929): 30.

The Woman at the Window [poem]. In *FSC*, *PM*. Evidently a poetic rendering of a prose poem of the same title (see p. 151).

The Woman at the Window [prose poem]. *Leaves* No. 2 (1938): 98–99. Wandrei mentions the work in a letter to Clark Ashton Smith (25 March 1927), hence was presumably written shortly before that date. For a versified rendering of the work, see "The Woman at the Window" (p. 81).

The Woodland Pool. In *E*, *PM*.

The Worm-King. *WT* 15, No. 6 (June 1930): 734. In *PM*.

You Will Come Back. In *DO*.

INDEX OF TITLES

Sanctity and Sin

Sanctity and Sin

INDEX OF FIRST LINES

Sanctity and Sin